International Organizations in Education

The importance of international organizations has dramatically increased since improved communications have made the term 'global village' more of a reality. Educationalists promote an essentially optimistic view of people and their capacities for control and change. Co-operation on an international scale in the field of education becomes a necessity and a major way forward if human progress is to be achieved in a world increasingly dominated by power struggles.

This collection of essays explores the various roles of international organizations in the field of adult education in particular. Two distinct categories emerge: organizations with a world-wide commitment, such as Unesco, and those with a more regional basis such as the African Association for Literacy and Adult Education. Each contributor examines the history and present characteristics of the organization before going on to consider possible future directions. The achievements and role of such organizations are considered, and each author offers a depth of personal experience. Together they reflect a range of opinion as varied as the parts of the world covered in the case studies.

Michael Stephens, the editor, is Robert Peers Professor of Adult Education at Nottingham University.

INTERNATIONAL ORGANIZATIONS IN EDUCATION

edited by

Michael D. Stephens

Routledge
London and New York

First published in 1988 by
Routledge
11 New Fetter Lane, London EC4P 4EE
29 West 35th Street, New York, NY 10001

©1989 M.D. Stephens

Typeset by LaserScript, Mitcham, Surrey
Printed and bound in Great Britain by
Biddles Ltd, Guildford and King's Lynn

British Library Cataloguing in Publication Data

International organizations in education.
   1. Adult education.   International organisations
   I. Stephens, Michael D. (Michael Dawson), *1936–*
374'.006'01
   ISBN 0-415-02183-9

Library of Congress Cataloging in Publication Data

International organizations in education / edited
   by Michael D. Stephens.
       p.   cm.
   Includes index.
   ISBN 0-415-02183-9
   1. Education--Societies, etc.   2. Adult education--Societies, etc.
   I. Stephens, Michael Dawson.
   L10.I8724   1989
   374'.006'01--dc19   88-22969
                                         CIP

For Margaret Knight of St Agnes

Contents

Contributors

TONY DELVES

Tony Delves began his teaching career in 1958 as an English and Social Studies teacher in secondary technical schools in Victoria, Australia. From 1963 to 1968 he was head of the Humanities Department at Prahran Technical School and became active in a number of committees in the field of English teaching. In 1963 he moved to the Curriculum and Research Branch of the Education Department, with responsibility for general curriculum development in secondary technical schools. During the period 1967–72 he published five English textbooks (together with W.G. Tickell) and *Issues in Teaching English* for Melbourne University Press. During that time and subsequently he wrote widely and spoke often, both on the teaching of English and on curriculum reform in the secondary school. In 1972 he became the founding principal of Huntingdale Technical School, a secondary technical school which quickly established a reputation as one of the most innovative schools in Australia. In 1979 the Australian College of Education conferred its fellowship on him, in recognition of his contribution to English teaching and secondary school leadership. In that year he was also appointed Director of Adult Education for the State of Victoria, with executive management responsibility for the Council of Adult Education. The Council of Adult Education was formed in 1946 as a statutory authority, and operates under the (revised) Council of Adult Education Act, 1981. It operates on a budget of A\$ 12 million per annum, provides support services to all adult education agencies in the state, and conducts programmes directly for 50,000 people a year. Its network of 45 local advisory committees in rural Victoria provides programmes for a further 50,000 people.

ETTORE GELPI

Ettore Gelpi studied at the University of Milan (Laurea in Constitutional Law) and at Teachers' College, Columbia University in New York (MA in Adult Education). Between 1956 and 1972 he worked in Italy in secondary, higher, adult, migrants', and union education. Since 1972 he has been Chief of the Lifelong Education Unit in Unesco, and since 1975 lecturer at the University of Paris. Among his publications are *Storia dell educazione* (History of Education, 1967); *Scuola senza cattedra* (School without Chair, 1969); *A Future for Lifelong Education* (1979); *Institutions et luttes éducatives* (Institutions and Educational Struggles, 1982); *Lifelong Education and International Relations* (1985).

BUDD HALL

Budd Hall is Secretary-General of the International Council for Adult Education. His BA and MA are from Michigan State University and his PhD from UCLA. During the 1960s and 1970s he had considerable experience of Africa and was Visiting Fellow at the Institute of Development Studies at the University of Sussex during 1974–5. From 1975 to 1979 he was Director of Research at the International Council before becoming Secretary-General. His publications on the education of adults are numerous.

DEREK LEGGE

Derek Legge was educated at the University of London, King's College, where he took a History degree and a Diploma in Education. He served for six years in the wartime army (five in army education). He became the University of Manchester's resident tutor in north-east Lancashire in 1946 and was appointed to the new Department of Adult Education at Manchester University in 1949, retiring as its head in 1976. Amongst his many publications has been *The Education of Adults in Britain* (1982). He was the first Individual Associate of the European Bureau of Adult Education.

LIM HOY PICK

Lim Hoy Pick obtained his BA from Nanyang University, Diploma in Education from the University of Singapore, and MA in Education from McGill University. He had been a high school teacher for four years before he joined the Department of Extra-Mural Studies, National University of Singapore. He is now the Director of the Department. He had been the Vice-President for

Asia of the International Council for Adult Education (ICAE) from 1983 to 1985. Now he is the President of the Asian-South Pacific Bureau of Adult Education (ASPBAE) and Chairman of ASPBAE Region 3.

JOHN LOWE

John Lowe is Head of the Country Educational Policy Reviews, Education and Training Division at OECD in Paris. He is a graduate of the University of Liverpool and holds a PhD from the University of London. He has been Director of Extra-Mural Studies at the University of Singapore, Director of the Department of Adult Education and Extra-Mural Studies at the University of Edinburgh, and Head of the Department of Educational Studies at the University of Edinburgh. He was appointed to his present post in 1973. His many publications in the field include *The Education of Adults: A World Perspective* (1975 and 1982).

ESMOND RAMESAR

Esmond Ramesar attended Mount Allison University, Canada (BSc), the University College of the West Indies, Jamaica (BSc), the Institute of Education, London (Postgraduate Certificate of Education), and the Ontario Institute for Studies in Education, Toronto (MEd). He was Senior Science Master, Wolmers' Boys' School, Jamaica (1958–60), Senior Science Master, Ghana College, Ghana (1960–3), Lecturer in Human Physiology/Pharmacology, College of Arts, Science and Technology, Jamaica (1963–4), Resident Tutor for Trinidad and Tobago, Department of Extra-Mural Studies, University of the West Indies (1964–7), CIDA Post-doctoral Fellow, OISE, University of Toronto (1967–9), Project Officer, Planning and Development Unit, UWI, Jamaica (1969–70), Tutor for Extra-Mural Studies, UWI, St Augustine, Trinidad (1970–80), and is now Director of Extra-Mural Studies, UWI, St Augustine (Trinidad) Campus (1980 to present). He has presented papers on different aspects of adult education at various international conferences and his publications include 'The status of scientific activity and the preconditions necessary for developing scientific literacy in the Commonwealth Caribbean: a critical approval', *Caribbean Issues* (1977); 'Recurrent issues in higher education in the Caribbean : a critical appraisal', in N.A. Niles and T. Gardener (eds) *Perspectives in West Indian Education* (1978); 'International and regional development in adult education', *Report of the Unesco Workshop on Adult Education and Literacy* (1983); 'Adult education: regional organisation in the Caribbean', *The International Encyclopedia of Education* (1985); and (with Leonard Shorey) 'Roby Kidd and the Caribbean', in N.J. Cochrane *et al.* (eds) *J.R. Kidd: An International Legacy of Learning* (1986).

ALAN ROGERS

Alan Rogers was on the staff of the Department of Adult Education, University of Nottingham, 1959–79; subsequently he became Professor of Continuing Education and Director of the Institute of Continuing Education at Magee University College, Londonderry. He has written extensively on local history and adult education, and has just published the book *Teaching Adults* (Open University Press). He is Secretary-General of the Commonwealth Association for the Education of Adults.

MOHI ELDINE SABER

Mohi Eldine Saber was born in 1919 at Dalgo in the Republic of the Sudan. He first studied there, then in Cairo, Paris, and Bordeaux. He holds a Doctor of Philosophy degree in anthropology from Cairo University and a Doctorat es-Lettres from l'Université de Bordeaux. He has occupied several posts in journalism and administration, and conducted university instruction in the Sudan (1954–9). He joined Unesco as Head of the Department of Social Sciences and Research at the centre of vocational education in Sers-al-lian, Egypt. In 1968 he was elected member of the Constituent Assembly in the Sudan and was, in the same year, appointed a member of the Senate of Khartoum University. In 1969 he was appointed Minister of Education and Higher Instruction. In 1973 he became President of ARLO (Arab Literacy Organization); associated with ALECSO (Arab League Educational, Cultural, and Scientific Organization). In 1976 the general assembly of ALECSO – constituted of the Arab ministers of education – elected Dr Saber Director-General of this organization which is considered to be the specialized agency in the field of education, culture, and sciences within the realm of the Arab League. He was re-elected to the post of Director-General of ALECSO for the period 1980–3, and further re-elected for the period 1984–7. Honorary doctor degrees have been bestowed upon Dr Saber by the Universities of Louvan, in Belgium, and Khartoum, in Sudan. He has also received decorations of merit from the Arab States of Sudan, Jordan Hashemite Kingdom, Islamic Republic of Mauritania, Peoples' Democratic Republic of Yemen, and the Arab Republic of Egypt, besides those from the Republics of Senegal, Chad, and France. His published works include *Cultural Change and Social Development* (first edition 1962, second edition 1986); *Research in Social Development Programmes* (1962); *Local Government and Social Development* (1966); *Bedouins and Nomadism: Concepts and Attitudes* (first edition 1966, second edition 1986); *Adult Education in the Sudan* (1969); *Modern Educational System in the Sudan* (1969); *Science of Adult Education* (1975); *Issues of Contemporary Arabic Culture* (1983); *Illiteracy: Problems and Solutions* (1985); *Readings in the Situation of Arab Culture* (1986); *Studies in Development and Adult Education Issues* (published by ARLO, Cairo, 1975; published in English under the title *Development and Adult Education in the Arab States* (edited by J.R. Kidd, published in Toronto, Canada, 1977).

MICHAEL D. STEPHENS

Michael D. Stephens has been the Robert Peers Professor of Adult Education at the University of Nottingham since 1974. He received his PhD from the University of Edinburgh. He has written frequently on the education of adults, travelled extensively, and been Research Fellow at the Johns Hopkins University, Visiting Scholar at Harvard, New Zealand Commonwealth Prestige Fellow, first Visiting Professor to the Council of Adult Education of Victoria (Australia), Consultant to the Australian Administrative Staff College, Japan Society for the Promotion of Science Fellow at the University of Kyoto, and Visiting Fellow at Yale.

EDWARD ULZEN

Edward Ulzen is from Ghana, West Africa. He was involved in education as Education Officer or Senior Education Officer from 1955 to 1960. He was Assistant Secretary in the Office of the President, Ghana, on the schedule of higher education 1960–2;

Registrar, University of Science and Technology, Ghana 1962–7; Senior Tutor/Lecturer in Adult Education, University of Zambia 1967–70; Registrar, University of Zambia 1970–3; Registrar, University of Botswana, Lesotho, and Swaziland Examinations Council 1973–4; Registrar, University of Botswana, Lesotho, and Swaziland 1974–5; Registrar (Special Duties) National University of Lesotho 1975–7; Executive Secretary, African Adult Education Association 1977–84; Executive Director, African Association for Literacy and Adult Education 1984–6. He has been involved in adult education as a volunteer, part-time and full-time, from 1950 to the present. He is also involved in the work and management of non-governmental organizations (NGOs). His current areas of interest in adult education are planning, administration, evaluation and project design, and implementation of NGOs.

Introduction

Michael D. Stephens

Since 1945 there has been an explosion of interest in international organizations. Many of the reasons for this are not difficult to see. There is the continuing revolution in transport; notably the arrival of effective air transport systems enabled representatives from a number of countries to meet with speed and relative ease in a chosen venue for the first time. The grim history of the twentieth century reinforced the belief that international communication would inhibit humankind's regular desire to wipe itself out. The increasing speed with which new knowledge in all fields appeared made national isolation costly. These, and many other factors, forced people to acknowledge that the term 'global village' was more than conference rhetoric. The new realities highlighted the inefficiency of last-ditch attempts to ignore the world outside a nation's boundaries.

Nowhere was the case for international organizations stronger than in the field of education. All countries since the Second World War have placed renewed emphasis on education. Economic and social improvement was seen as requiring a literate and numerate citizenry. Once this had been largely achieved in a country there followed an increase in demand for further and higher education. Inevitably such developments were accompanied by the employment of much larger numbers of professional teachers and educational administrators. A professional educationalist usually has an interest in how others tackle the field. He or she is quick to recognize the greater impact co-operation can have in solving a problem or pressuring a government for the implementation of desirable change. To state the obvious the professional has more time available to devote to the international dimension of education.

Many of these points are to be found in the following essays. These all deal with various agencies within the field of the education of adults. Adult education has been chosen because it is more manageable than trying to deal with the whole of education, but illustrates most of the major characteristics of international organizations in this area. It is also frequently wracked by self-doubt and so asks more searching questions of itself than is the case with, say, child-based education. Such questions will permit the reader to appreciate the arguments for and against international organizations.

In fact Edward Ulzen ends his chapter with the question 'Is a regional organization necessary?' His response to this is revealing for he is careful to stress that such international organizations cannot 'accomplish what is best done by a national association or government department at a national level'. He suggests that the African Adult Education Association had

> been able to sensitize public opinion and governments of Africa to the bane of illiteracy; provided advocacy for literacy and adult education before governments; mobilized qualified and interested persons to give freely of their time, expertise, and service to the cause; created a forum for exchange of experiences and innovative methods for the benefit of practitioners in the service of governments in the region; and had given training to trainers of trainers for work in their different countries.

Similar points are made by Derek Legge when writing of the European Bureau:

> Its role in promoting contact and co-operation between educators of adults, and in providing opportunities for the exchange of ideas and the creation of real fellowship, is now more than ever vital. In the technologically advanced world of today with its ever-increasing speed of change, adult educators, in adjusting their work, can be greatly helped by an awareness of the changes in purposes, organization, and methods which are in progress in other countries.

Outside this volume, a major contribution has been made by Richard H. Henstrom of Brigham Young University, USA, who, in a carefully researched paper given to the Comparative Adult Education Conference at Oxford in July 1987, reported on his review of some sixty international and national official statements on adult education. These declarations included such well-known ones as those for the Unesco Conferences at Elsinore (1949), Montreal (1960), Tokyo (1972), Nairobi (1976), and Paris (1985). Most of the examples are national ones, but there are common areas of interest. Henstrom lists specific educational statements in most of the following areas: political; social; cultural; economic (vocational emphasis); remedial (literacy emphasis); health; democratization; peace; general-aesthetic education; recreational-leisure education; self-realization or self-fulfilment; ethics-values (moral); basic education; religious life.

Henstrom also indicated that there were groups which international organizations saw as needing particular attention such as women; elderly people; workers; disabled people; illiterates; the family; immigrants and ethnic minorities; unemployed people; oppressed and disadvantaged people; and prisoners. Henstrom included the warning about international organizations,

> Goals and objectives are often idealistic and lofty. . . . It also needs to be understood that there is usually a gap between statements of philosophy and objectives and the reality of actual achievement. The practice in the field may not always coincide with the statements of intent or desire.

We have come a long way since the World Association for Adult Education was founded in 1919, but educationalists in all fields can be bewitched by empty rhetoric. What is irrefutable is that developments in human affairs make lifelong education unavoidable for increasingly large numbers of people who find their initial education, if they were fortunate enough to have any, inadequate to function effectively in modern societies. As adult education becomes rapidly more important the priorities listed by international organizations are more pressing. The rhetoric has to be harnessed to the reality.

Alan Rogers in writing about the Commonwealth reminds us that education can be seen by some countries as less significant than, say, economic development. As he points out, the Commonwealth Secretariat employs a staff of some four hundred of which the Education Division accounts for nine. Then again at any particular moment in time an issue may dominate a region and its organizations such as the nuclear debate in the South Pacific during much of 1986 and 1987. While education continues to be of importance it finds itself overshadowed, if only temporarily, by such an issue. Despite this, new international organizations to promote education continue to arise. For example the International League for Social Commitment in Adult Education had its founding conference in June 1984 and has since grown rapidly. Its seven objectives reveal much about the international audience sought:

Objective 1 To encourage all those involved in adult education to foster participation in dialogue on the critical social issues confronting humankind today, such as class inequality, environmental concerns, peace, racism, sexism, and ageism.

Objective 2 To encourage all those involved in adult education to identify and act to overcome the social, political, and economic forces which perpetuate the existence of poverty, oppression, and political powerlessness.

Objective 3 To encourage all those in adult education to view and practise adult education as a vehicle to enable all adults to gain and exert control over their own lives.

Objective 4 To encourage all those involved in adult education to work with the poor, oppressed, and politically powerless in learning activities which have social, political, economic, cultural, and aesthetic import.

Objective 5 To encourage all adult educators to make explicit the ethics and values that guide their practice.

Objective 6 To encourage those responsible for the preparation of adult educators to provide not only for the enhancement of technical skills, but also for the critical examination of ethical and social issues.

Objective 7 To encourage the design, conduct, and reporting of research and other forms of scholarship focusing on adult education as a force for social change.

Despite a number of roles which are also served by other international organizations the International League obviously brings a distinctive quality to its contribution which is not paralleled by the former. However, its proposed machinery shares much in common with such groupings with a biennial general meeting as a focus. Its 1986 Conference at the University of Nottingham lists 'work towards developing mechanisms to facilitate the exchange of ideas, knowledge, and resources among members and other concerned individuals and organizations'.

Most long-lasting international organizations reach a stage where it becomes apparent that full-time staff are needed to reinforce existing achievements and to enable further expansion to take place. This tendency is well illustrated by Edward Ulzen's account of the African Adult Education Association:

The establishment of the Association's secretariat in 1976 with the support of the International Council for Adult Education and funding by the Canadian International Development Agency, occurred within the context of a region, the attention of whose governments and people had been focused on adult education. The secretariat immediately planned to promote the formation of national associations of its members throughout sub-Saharan Africa; to bring the knowledge of its existence, objectives, and programmes to all African governments and organizations; to develop training programmes for regional and sub-regional workshops involving practitioners and middle-level adult education workers; to create networks of communication between agencies, trainers, and practitioners; and to undertake studies and research in adult education and publish their results as well as provide a forum for exchange of information.

Such an ambitious programme of expansion could not be expected to reach all its targets. Virtually all international organizations find their resources do not match their programmes.

Adult education suffers such shortages to a degree not found in most school-based systems. Lim Hoy Pick illustrates aspects of this dilemma:

In spite of the growing realization among Asian countries of its crucial importance, adult education was still restricted to a marginal position in regard to the national education system. This marginality of adult education resulted from various factors. Modern educational systems in Asia were primarily modelled upon those of the western nations. Compared to the formal education, adult education was introduced to Asia at a much later date. Immediately after the Second World War, several countries in Asia gained their national independence. This was followed by a baby boom in the 1950s which resulted in an overwhelmingly large young population in the newly independent nations and the urgent need of education for the young became the prime concern of the governments. Another important contributing factor to marginality seemed to be the lack of adequate institutional structures and shortage of professionally trained adult education personnel.

A majority of the international organizations described in this book have had the training of such adult educators as a priority.

Mohi Saber brings home the pressing nature of such training needs when he points out that the Iraqi literacy campaign recruited 73,000 teachers in 18 months. As John Lowe in his pioneering book *Adult Education and Nation Building* (Edinburgh University Press, 1970) stated, 'The lack of qualified adult educators is frequently referred to, and indeed for adult education planners the provision of appropriate training facilities may well be the most pressing of all their problems'. It would appear that progress in this key area has been less than was hoped for. The Caribbean Community Secretariat Seminar/Workshop held in St Lucia in 1977 recognized this in its two recommendations, which are reported by Esmond Ramesar in his description of the establishing of the Caribbean Regional Council for Adult Education. These suggested the establishing of a Commission for Adult Education, and 'that the training of adult educators within the region should be viewed as a matter of priority'.

Ettore Gelpi makes the important point that amongst the categories of international organization it is possible to see two major divisions of co-operation, namely that of the industrial countries and also for the developing states of the world. The former is notably characterized by technological and scientific transfers. The latter Gelpi sees as concentrating mainly on 'pedagogical traditional activities'. He also highlights the two long-established patterns of co-operation. There is the 'humanitarian aid' of the west to the south, and the 'ideological fraternity' of the east towards the south. In reality the west receives more from the south in material terms than it gives, and the relationship of such countries as the Soviet Union with the south is too often seen as that of an arms supplier. Where international organizations attempt to take an independent and democratic line they invariably face pressure from either the western or eastern blocs. Unesco's pariah image in the USA and Britain of recent years certainly owed something to this. Washington and London found uncongenial the directions favoured by a majority, largely Third World, of Unesco's membership.

Countries with superior economic power have always attempted to impose their will on weaker or smaller nations. International organizations during the past have been established to protect the less powerful. Of late the economic differences between, say, the USA and Uganda have become even more pronounced. Technological developments have given the former even greater tools for domination. The field of information technology alone equips the USA with previously unheard-of power. These developments make international forums of more importance than ever before. Alas, it is usually the economic, military, or educational nationalism which dominates. Co-operation remains less effective than a safe future of the world needs.

However, educationalists have a need to be optimists. As Budd Hall states,

> We are beginning to have the structures to share what we are hearing on an international level. With support and encouragement and a little bit of luck we have the chance to build for ourselves an international movement which believes in people and their capacities for control and change.

The apparently tenuous way in which humankind hangs on to survival on this planet may just be improving a little. The creation of so many international organizations could be an indicator that the Berlin Bunker approach to world affairs has passed as an era. Countries and their leaders are less intent on getting their way or else exiting amidst a holocaust. States with dominating economic and military power still wish to direct others along their favoured paths, but seem more willing to come to terms with failure. The world remains a very dangerous place, but there is evidence to encourage we optimists.

Such thoughts bring to centre stage the questions raised by Tony Delves in Chapter 1. Do international organizations assist adults in obtaining the learning they need? Are such terms as 'lifelong learning', much favoured in international forums, mere conference rhetoric? What do delegates bring to such organizations, and what do they take away? Regarding this point there is some evidence to support the cynic's view that there are international jet-setters who grace every gathering with little to contribute and only their surplus expenses to take away. This is patently not true of the bulk of those involved in the initiatives of international organizations, but they do exist and are not a phenomenon only of the developed world. Perhaps Tony Delves's most fundamental question relating to international organizations is 'Would the world of adult education be any different without them?' Both his essay and the following ones suggest that it would.

Part 1

Setting the scene

1

The professional's view of international organizations in education

Tony Delves

It began with my induction to the Information Group.

I knew that the head of the Australian delegation (a career diplomat with, fortunately, a strong background in education) to the Fourth Unesco International Conference on Adult Education (Paris, March 1985) seemed to slip off from time to time to meetings which were not part of the formal agenda. So when he was called away for a few days by his 'boss' he asked me if I would attend meetings of the Information Group for him. It turned out to be a meeting forum for 'friendly western powers' aimed at discussing and influencing the progress of the Conference and, in particular, the wording of the various recommendations. I assume that other groups of 'friendly powers' had similar meetings.

This was, then, my first (and probably only) foray into the realms of international diplomacy. I was summoned to my first meeting in true James Bond fashion by a whisper in my ear from a friendly female power, 'Information Group, Room so-and-so, 1600 hours'. It was clear that nearby not-so-friendly powers were not meant to hear. All-in-all I attended three or four meetings. Although impressed with the fervour of the discussions, I understood very little of what was going on. Certainly it did not seem to have much to do with adult education. The main theme was clearly politics: the chief obsession was with the *words* used in the draft recommendations. Some of the people who attended did not seem to take any other part in the Conference proceedings. By my second meeting various theories were beginning to emerge about why the world is in the mess it is. And these were the *friendly* western powers!

One example will, I hope, suffice. One phrase – I think it was 'peace and international development' – was repeated in a number of draft recommendations from some other set of powers. We were told by the chairman (British, but I have no idea who he was or how he got there, or even if he was a delegate – he certainly was not an adult educator) that this phrase was *unacceptable* as it stood because it had some special meaning in international diplomacy which, if we accepted it, would hand an important victory to another set of powers. In this context, a careful review of the draft recommendations also revealed the phrase 'peace in the world'. The chairman immediately said, 'Hold on, this is a new one. It will have to go.' Half-audibly, and with full intent, I said, 'Jesus Christ', and laughed. Those around me looked at me as if I was mad. Perhaps they are right, but I wonder if any of them have ever read Kafka.

Fortunately my feelings about the Information Group were shared by my leader and by another member of the Australian delegation who accompanied me to one of the meetings to make sure I wasn't dreaming. The Report of the Australian Delegation to our government included the following:

> The Information Group met frequently during the second week of the Conference. Many delegates commented on the politicising effect of these meetings particularly with regard to the final plenary. Although the political aspects of draft recommendations in particular are important it could be said that the presence of trained political officers in discussions on adult education may have the effect of introducing and highlighting political points which could be more usefully handled in a low key manner. Two western representatives who took a leading part in the final session of this meeting were not members of their official delegations. The session may have proceeded more smoothly if they had confined themselves to advising their delegations who could then have handled [the issues] as educationists.
>
> (*Report of Australian Delegation* 1985: 12, para. 49)

This whole experience has led me to reflect deeply, and somewhat negatively, on the pitfalls of internationalism in adult education.

Not that the warning signs hadn't been there.

Three years earlier I had spent three months or so looking at the provision of adult education in the United Kingdom and various other European countries. It seemed not unreasonable that I should visit both Unesco and OECD in Paris to learn something of the role of these international agencies in adult education. Arranging such visits was more difficult than I had thought. Although preliminary letters were sent some six months before I left Australia, no replies were forthcoming and I was forced to complete arrangements after I had arrived in Europe. Even at this distance in time this seems to be more than a little odd, unless, of course, these agencies are so inundated with mail that they cannot answer it all.

Of course it may also be that meeting with the head of a state (i.e. Victoria) government (rather than national) adult education authority from a distant and, from their perspective, not very important country takes rather low priority. I had, perhaps naively, thought that I would learn a great deal from each agency and that they would be interested in the work of my authority, which also happens to be a very large provider of adult education programmes by world standards. I was wrong on both counts.

Put at its most cynical, I travelled 20,000 kilometres to spend an hour in one agency, forty-five minutes in the other – not so much as a cup of tea or coffee – in idle chit-chat. The people themselves were fine and friendly, but they seemed to be living in a world which had almost no relevance to the provision of adult education to the people of my state. I left wondering, and it was that same sense of wondering which partly overcame me again in Paris in 1985.

It would be too easy, too glib, to discuss international organizations on the strength of a couple of anecdotes. The justification for such organizations rests on far firmer ground: the need for international co-operation across a range of important issues in adult education; the need for professionals with a common cause to be able to work together and to provide mutual support; the need to have routes by which to address international issues, but which bypass the normal political processes.

There are very sound reasons for the existence of a number of adult education international organizations, and the extraordinary altruism of many who founded, or who work in, them is widely recognized. Why, then, do I feel some unease? Partly it arises out of what I will call *international style* and partly out of questions of *relevance* and *impact*.

3

In a way, it is the matter of international style which has struck me most: a style not generated by adult education as such and, in fact, quite negative in its influence on the much more important issues which face the adult education community world-wide.

One of the oddities of attending international conferences is the ease with which it is possible to adopt a form of address which ascribes both to you and to your words a status which they simply do not have. The key words which signal this phenomenon are, in my case, 'In Australia we believe . . .' or 'Australia takes the view that . . . '. Perhaps this mode of presentation is justified in some forums – for example, the United Nations General Assembly – or for some countries, but there is a great danger in adult education that such statements become overly pretentious, being at best inaccurate and at worst absurd.

Certainly to speak of a coherent view of adult education in Australia is especially difficult. It is impossible to do so without taking into account the variations both between and within states. The Australian Government itself has no considered approach to adult education, although it occasionally scatters a few dollars over the continent for such programmes as literacy and basic education. Hence, 'In Australia, we . . . ' immediately rings alarm bells in my head when it is applied to adult education.

The chief danger, of course, is of gross superficiality. In 1982 following my extensive study tour, I wrote a report, *Reflections on an Overseas Study Tour*, on what I had seen. The focus of the report was primarily on relating what I had seen to the potential for improvement in my own organization and state. However, as I re-read the report now, I am also struck by how easily I slipped into the same superficial process: 'Yet throughout Europe I was disappointed at the dull and unimaginative programs which were being offered through the formal adult education agencies'. In Australia we become upset very quickly when some, often minimally informed, overseas visitor passes through and then pronounces judgement. If I were writing my 1982 report again it would still be forthright but much more guarded in approach. The problem, in retrospect, was that I had slipped too easily into an *international style*: I had assumed the cloak of an *expert*.

In various Australian and overseas travels before and after 1982, the phenomenon of the 'international expert' has always intrigued me. The style overwhelms the person; internationalism takes precedence over the realities of adult education. Of their nature, international organizations carry this danger, especially amongst those who are most active in them.

This problem was thrown up at the 1985 Unesco Conference in a most unusual form, but in a way which highlights the danger. The Drafting Group, appointed to consolidate the plethora of draft recommendations, quickly pointed out that it needed the capacity to synthesize and to negotiate rewording of similar recommendations from different delegations. This procedure, of course, appealed to all the adult educators as it accorded with normal adult education practice in such circumstances. Yet it was opposed by the Unesco Secretariat on the grounds that it was breaking some rule or set procedure. Fortunately the Conference overruled the Secretariat and common sense prevailed. Although the Secretariat consisted of a number of leading adult educators, it had, in what I am sure was a brief moment of aberration, put their procedures on some kind of higher-order plane than either the Conference or the principles of adult education. Internationalism had, for a few hours, become an end for itself, totally detached from the reality of the Conference or the world.

In the same vein, I have some unease about the way in which international organizations have taken on the structures and titles of the international market-place. One would hope that the newly formed Commonwealth Association for the Education and Training of Adults might look afresh at such matters, although early indications are that it might well follow uncritically down the same path. I note, for example, the easy acceptance of the term 'Secretary General' and of a constitution which, with the best will in the world, may turn out to be over-complicated and perhaps unworkable.

However, of much greater importance than matters of style are those of substance. Do international organizations have relevance to and impact on the lives of those for whom adult education exists, the adult population? Certainly there is great potential for such organizations to act as agents for change, as reinforcement of things well done, as spurs for things done badly or not at all. It would be superficial indeed to attempt to pass judgement on their effectiveness on those grounds. Perhaps, then, it might be more pertinent to sketch out some of the questions which such organizations need to be asking themselves.

How do such organizations contribute to ensuring that the actual learning needs of adults are met? Is 'lifelong learning' a term used by academics, policy-makers, and organizations as a form of rhetoric or is there substance, and progress, in real achievement?

What do delegates bring to organizations and, more importantly, what do they take away? How do the organizations help in reducing the gulf between the haves and the have-nots? How do they help resolve the dilemmas inherent in the vocational/non-vocational aspects of adult education? What actual contribution do they make to effecting change? Can they do more than merely publicize needs, issues, and ideas? Who, apart from the direct participants, actually benefits from their work? Would the world of adult education be any different without them?

Such organizations also need to develop sound strategies for influencing governments. On the experience of the 1985 Unesco Conference it is clear that many delegates looked for strong affirming statements about the role of adult education as something that could be used to positive effect in their own countries. Hence the statement 'The Right to Learn', put forward by the Canadian delegation, was widely applauded by the Conference. As a statement, it took the high moral ground of adult education, as can be seen from its concluding paragraph:

> Who will decide what humanity will become in the future? This is the question facing all governments, non-governmental organizations, individuals and groups. This, too, is the question facing the women and men who are working in adult education and who seek to enable all people, ranging from individuals to groups to humanity as a whole, to gain control of themselves and of their own destiny.

Similar sentiments, in briefer form, became the Declaration from the ICAE World Assembly of Adult Education in November 1985 in Buenos Aires. It is difficult to see how one could argue against them. It is even more difficult to discern the *actual* impact on the national governments to which they are directed. I can see no evidence, in Australia, of governments being even remotely affected by them, although our politicians would no doubt claim that we are already doing all those good things sought so earnestly in such statements.

How do international organizations contribute to the key issues in adult education? For vast numbers of people, the key issue is literacy. In Asia and the South Pacific alone, the number of post-school illiterates now exceeds 650 million, and the number is rising. In international forums this issue dominates the agenda of many nations, and understandably so. Literacy has become fundamental not merely to living but as an agent of positive social change. How do we provide a constant and comprehensive literacy programme which meets personal and social needs, is derived from local and regional cultures, and contributes to economic and political life? Where do the organizations stand on this issue? What is their contribution to its resolution? How do we in our comfortable western cultures, with important but nevertheless relatively slight literacy problems, cope with a single issue of such magnitude on a global scale?

Part of the answer may lie in technology: the achievement of variety and diversity of learning forms and methods, with the capacity to cross national and international boundaries, which technology allows. Another, to develop long-term strategies so that there is continuity and growth, starting with literacy, rather than the world-wide repetition of safe, conventional courses and programmes.

Can the disparate thrusts of government policies at various times and in various countries be brought together to sustain the movement we have called 'adult education'? In a single cross-world conversation we can be using the term to mean self-development in the liberal tradition, social reform, leisure activities, vocational education through skill training, literacy, and community development – or any combination of these things. Can international organizations help to clarify these issues and the links between them?

How do they contribute to the work of non-governmental organizations (NGOs)? There is a substantial emphasis on NGOs in the international arena, for reasons which are not entirely clear. In Australia at least, such organizations have become more heavily dependent on government funds as a way of meeting part of their costs. What has become essential is to develop a balance between direct government provision and the role of NGOs. There is a long tradition of unpaid community work in adult education and this must not only be valued in its own right but also support, and be supported by, government provision.

Perhaps because I work in a government agency, I sometimes feel that the role of NGOs is overstated in international organizations. On the other hand, I also know that the value of their work, and of the myriad unpaid workers in adult education, cannot be overstated. The solution may be to promote diversity and flexibility of provision as key elements, and to insist that both governments and NGOs have a key collective role to play. I noted with great interest the suggestion of a UK delegate at the 1985 Unesco Conference that there may be a need for new kinds of partnerships between governments and NGOs, perhaps based on contractual arrangements between them. This is a pathway that has already emerged, and been found to be particularly fruitful, in my own state. Can international organizations foster such joint-enterprise approaches?

In the end, the need for international organizations in adult education probably rests on the need for us all, in the midst of varied and difficult social, cultural, and economic circumstances, to be better informed so that we'might assist one another. Although this same rationale can be equally applied across a vast spectrum of human activities, it somehow assumes particular importance for adult educators. In essence, such organizations also provide a unique opportunity to further our own adult education.

If, however, international organizations become obsessed with structures and procedures, the possibilities for action, on either a regional or global scale, diminish accordingly. If the major conferences become swamped by political considerations they will quickly lose their value and adult education will have become yet another slogan to wave above the political bandstand. Out of the grand words, the meetings, the masses of paper must come programmes, processes, and services which are real to those in need. If international organizations can add, even in small measure, to that reality they will have succeeded: if not, their continuing existence must be seriously questioned.

REFERENCES

Delves, T. (1982) *Reflections on an Overseas Study Tour: April–August 1982*, Melbourne: Council of Adult Education.
—— *Report of Australian Delegation, Unesco Fourth International Conference on Adult Education, Paris 19–29 March 1985.*

2

Education, international relations, and co-operation

Ettore Gelpi

GOVERNMENTAL AND NON-GOVERNMENTAL INTERNATIONAL AGENCIES

In the past, between countries, education was supported through military interventions, religious missions, and ideological inculcations. These instruments of 'educational co-operation' are still operating between countries, but new mechanisms are developing because new international relations are emerging.

International governmental and non-governmental, bilateral and multilateral, organizations have developed since 1945: Unesco with its main responsibilities in the field of education, culture, and science – and in the 1960s also the International Bureau of Education (IBE) joined Unesco – the Food and Agriculture Organization (FAO) with components in education as far as training in the field of agriculture is concerned; the International Labour Organization (ILO) with responsibilities in the field of education as far as industrial relations and training are concerned; and the World Health Organisation (WHO) with relevant training programmes for hygiene, prevention of disease, and training of medical and health personnel.

It is interesting to know the new names of the agencies of the traditional industrial countries: from colonial development and welfare acts, and from overseas territories' agencies, to service of technical co-operation, to creation of ministers of overseas development agencies. And second, the emergence of technical co-operation agencies of new industrial countries from the north and from the south.

As far as international inter-governmental agencies are concerned, further specific agencies were created in the 1960s and the 1970s to support educational and training activities in the very different fields of agriculture and industry: UNDP (1965), UNIDO (1967), IFAD (1977), and so on. The World Bank is also increasing its activities in the field of education.

During the last forty years, the imbalance between educational needs and educational and cultural co-operation increased both because of the increased educational demand of the great majority of countries on one side, and because of a more limited interest of developed nations to offer international co-operation in the field of education, when a mild competition started between the north and some southern countries, on the other side.

As far as international governmental organizations were concerned, their activities were concentrated mainly in the so-called less developed countries and they became more dependent on bilateral aid for those educational projects requiring important financial contributions.

THE NATURE OF INTERNATIONAL CO-OPERATION

We have the impression that two different types of international co-operation are developing in the field of education: one for the industrial countries (within the west and within the east, and among east and west), another one for developing countries (for the south from the north). The first co-operation is developing mostly through scientific and technological information, intellectual exchange, and sometimes common projects. And the second co-operation is concentrated mostly on pedagogical traditional activities (if there are technological and scientific transfers, they are not reflecting the most interesting innovations).

On the contrary it would be important to forecast real international co-operation in the field of education without grading education only through the amount of educational expenditure of this or that country or this or that region. Education and culture cannot be judged in relation to GNP, or only technological achievements, or on quantitative formal, educational, and cultural consumption.

Since 1945 the forty-three years of work of inter-governmental, international, governmental, and non-governmental agencies deserve to be evaluated, looking at the positive and negative aspects. Light and shadows belong to this history. It is clear that international co-operation played a useful role in some emergency situations, during the first years of decolonization and because of the very dramatic living conditions of different countries. And the contribution was also positive because these international agencies had the ability to diffuse relevant educational innovations. But the shadows were also numerous: first, the one-way co-operation with educational donors and receivers (formally few educational innovations moved from the south to the north, but fortunately in the real-life situation it was different); second, this educational co-operation was always kept in a low profile (the risk of a real educational exchange often was not taken) because of the fear of competition; third, international educational co-operation compares very poorly with international military co-operation; fourth, a divided technological world implies a divided educational co-operation (nevertheless, some countries of the north, of the south, and of the southern part of the north, are becoming a bridge and a place where educational exchanges are taking place because, at the same time, exchange of technologies is developing).

CRISIS, RESISTANCES, AND HOPES

The crisis of bilateral and international co-operation is the result of the crisis of two previous patterns of co-operation: west towards south through 'charity' and 'humanitarian aid' and east towards south through 'ideological fraternity'. Both models are disappointing. Northern countries are receiving more money than they are giving to southern countries; 'ideological fraternity' has some difficulties in being convincing because it is more and more associated with weapons (so-called military assistance or selling of arms or wars against southern people). And new positive contradictions are arising: some religious groups are no longer a tool for domination but on the contrary are becoming a reference for independence; political groups of certain countries refuse to be a belt of transmission of a pre-packed ideology and are structuring themselves as political movements geared to the self-management of their societies.

International governmental and non-governmental structures are under attack when they try to develop independent policies of a democratic nature; the most powerful countries of the east and west try to give a low profile to international structures when they face a refusal to obey. Unfortunately sometimes international structures, governmental and non-governmental, through bureaucratic and arrogant ways, try to impose educational and cultural models often taken from some of the leading countries.

Within the same country civilian society can oppose violence or absence of the state structures; within the framework of international institutions, when they are too authoritarian or absent, it is difficult to find a civilian international society able to resist, and to complement the public international institutions. Local and national life, self-managed initiatives, independent and creative struggles for education and culture have difficulties to find their correspondence in other societies in order to create international resistance or co-operation, but the building of an international civilian society is the most challenging and concrete project for the end of this century and the following one. The construction of an international civilian society depends on politics and educational content. But to what extent is the aim of the construction of an international civilian society taken into consideration? To what extent are the countries of the centre making a systematic effort to make known different cultures and to inform about the new social, cultural, scientific, and technological dynamics? To what extent do the elites in the Third World countries want to, or can, make known the relations of dependence imposed on their countries?

Because of the difficulties of a complete control of peripheral countries and because of the struggle among big powers in the economic and political domain, we are witness to an international division of the influence of the most powerful states on different international organizations dealing with educational and cultural matters. The technicalities are sometimes very sophisticated to enable the open or hidden 'masters' to wear an international mask and at the same time to impede a one-dimensional educational and cultural approach.

For example, non-formal education is supported by countries who want to reduce public education; unidimensional formal education is supported by countries who fear mass creativity and like a dominating central control. But people (and peripheral countries) want to have both formal and non-formal education. In my international working experience, once I tried to invite to an international meeting Andrei Wajda, the famous Polish movie-maker, who, to me, is an expression of a creative non-formal education. I was told there was no room for this creator in a meeting on lifelong education. When a meeting was called in Unesco for the anniversary of Karl Marx's death, on one side the USA protested and on the other side the USSR and a few other planned-economies countries sent only official researchers, but the very lively independent Marxist researchers of these countries were not allowed to take part in the meeting.

The dialectics between progressive and reactionary forces are multifacetted: minority groups in the north are fighting within their own countries to develop more equitable relations between north and south; in some countries of the south, people are still working to liberate themselves from ancient and new colonizations. The best way for the reactionary people in the north (east and west) is to make alliances in the south with groups that they are controlling through military and financial aid. These complex relations often have relevant educational implications such as training abroad, fellowships, and associations with specific professional organizations. The independent progressive researchers, intellectuals, and leaders in the southern countries have difficulties in profiting from the international communication, because they do not accept becoming dependent on established channels of communication and training.

Education is becoming more and more relevant in international relations because it is strongly related to the transfer of the technologies of training and communication software. Powerful countries are using education to make a new impact and control on more peripheral countries.

THE MILITARY COMPONENTS

The internationalization of arms and of military structures has also significant consequences for education at several levels: on one side there are new elaborate technologies (the arms industry and the military organization are often transferred to civilian production) and on the other side, in different societies, the military play a major role in political and administrative matters.

The internationalization of military power has also strong implications on education that is related to this internationalization, because powerful countries are providers of technologies, weapons, and training for many armies of the developing countries.

Educationalists do not pay so much attention to the influence of military co-operation in education. On the contrary, historically, and today also, this influence is very strong. Today, as in previous centuries, military people exercise a relevant educational role because they impose models and educational content to a significant part of the present and future ruling class. But how are armies contributing to international relations? Peripheral countries are not so eager to, or they cannot, evaluate this contribution. Dialectically we can say that solidarity against military invasion of peripheral countries is an important educational contribution to the new international relations.

EDUCATION AND DEVELOPMENT

The idea to relate education to development is a positive one. But often developmental education supports models that are openly or secretly imposed from outside. The 1950s and the 1960s reflected the idea of one development that was necessary for all countries; the 1970s and the 1980s reflected another approach consisting in some kind of segregation recognizing that different countries have to develop differently in relation to their history and to their modern possibilities. In both cases, the approaches of development had a negative influence on international educational co-operation because countries were graded giving them different developmental status.

Training and technology transfers are becoming an important dimension of production. These transfers are dangerous if the cultural and educational identity of individuals and peoples are not respected; transfers can even be complementary if identity does not mean a petrified culture and they are not an instrument of domination.

But the great omission in international educational co-operation is often culture, because of its revolutionary nature. Educators often ignore the cultural realities behind the educational activities. Culture can lead to creation and allows reality to be seen through the eyes of painters and musicians and not only through those of the accountants. Culture can stimulate motivation to understand other people and to produce the pleasure of participating in the transformation of society. Culture can also be creative participation – a participation of users and performers in the different arts.

THE ACTORS

National states and international organizations are not the only actors of education in international relations: other non-formal actors are playing relevant roles in this respect. To give some examples: migrants, media, visual, and performing arts experts can be involved.

Migrants are very often excellent animators of cultural and educational activities leading to international relations; sometimes this animation faces strong opposition, sometimes it is smooth. Native populations of northern countries often reject or oppose external and cultural influences. But even in this opposition native people are obliged to take into consideration and know better such diversity. And, at the same time, even among those who refuse culture and education from outside, it is possible to assist very interesting forms of education and cultural development through models of leisure time, of cooking, and of social relations, introduced by migrants. On the other side, native populations are influencing the education of second-generation migrants and new international relations and sometimes confrontations develop within relevant urban communities.

Fast technological development and technological mobility also mean relevant education for international relations through exported expertise and imported learners. Exported experts can contribute positively or negatively to international relations, due to the quality of the expertise and to their cultural sensitivity and awareness. Foreign students can play a positive or negative role in international communication, and also in this case, their cultural identity is relevant for positive communication, avoiding external domination.

International education is the work of people: educators, researchers, administrators, policy-makers. Their world identity is important for the development of a meaningful international educational and cultural exchange. Unfortunately this identity finds some difficulty in being created: world consciousness is not yet a reality in institutions when countries are often fighting each other at the military, technological, and economic levels.

Part 2

International organizations

3

Inter-governmental organizations in education

John Lowe

STRUCTURES AND FUNCTIONS

This chapter is concerned with the role in education of the more important inter-governmental organizations: the Council of Europe (CDCC); the Organization for Economic Co-operation and Development (OECD); the United Nations Educational, Scientific and Cultural Organization (Unesco); and the World Bank (the Bank). It is proposed to describe the structure and functions of each one, to examine the similarities and differences among them, and to appraise their strong and weak points and overall achievement.

Inter-governmental organizations are a twentieth-century phenomenon. They were few and largely ineffectual before the Second World War and, in any case, only marginally concerned with education. Since 1945, however, their number has multiplied and several have come to attach greater or less priority to educational affairs.

Unesco, which belongs to the United Nations family, was founded in 1946 against the background of idealism and optimism about the future of international co-operation that characterized the immediate post-war period. It was designed to represent states, that is to be expressly an inter-governmental rather than simply an international organization. All states, regardless of their size or economic productivity, were to have equal constitutional rights. The initial membership of 44 countries had increased to 161 by the end of 1987. As proclaimed in the very title of Unesco, education, perceived as the key to international understanding, was to be the first priority, although it was clearly intended from the outset that science and culture would be indissolubly bound to it. The functions of Unesco, according to its charter, are to assist countries in the development of their educational services, to foster a regular exchange of ideas and information, and to arrange foreign visits for professional experts.

Unesco's programmes are formally determined and sanctioned by a General Conference that assembles every two years. It is controlled continually by an executive board of thirty-four members that meets twice a year. Day-to-day activities are carried out by a permanent secretariat under the supervision of a director-general, appointed by the general conference, who wields substantial powers. Revenue is provided by member countries, each contributing according to the size of its gross domestic product (GDP). Some technical assistance programmes are financed from other sources, notably from the United Nations Development Programme (UNDP). Many non-governmental organizations have been granted affiliated status.

The *CDCC* is socalled because the educational and cultural activities of the Council of Europe are directly controlled by the Council for Cultural Co-operation (created in 1962) and supervised by two committees for General and Technical Education and for Out-of-School Education and Sport respectively. The CDCC comprises twenty-three member states, two of which – Finland and the Holy See – do not belong to the Council of Europe. Its main aims are

1   to encourage the development of lifelong education;
2   to assist in the improvement and democratization of education;
3   to pay special attention to the educational needs of immigrants;
4   to arouse general awareness in member countries of the place of Europe in the world.

The highlight of the CDCC's programme is the biennial meeting of the Standing Conference of European Ministers of Education; the initial meeting took place in 1961. Preparations are carried out by the permanent secretariat under the supervision of a 'Committee of Senior Officials' representing national ministries of education. The whole programme is financed out of the 'Cultural Fund', which was instituted in 1954.

OECD evolved in 1961 out of the Organization for European Economic Co-operation that had been established in 1948 to administer Marshall Aid. It comprises twenty-four countries and is sometimes referred to as 'the rich man's club'; its main aim is to promote the economic well-being of its member countries. It is governed by a council consisting of the permanent representatives of each member country. Meetings of the council are chaired by a secretary-general, who also heads the permanent secretariat. The council meets annually at ministerial level and on that occasion member countries are represented by ministers of finance, foreign affairs, and trade. The activities of OECD are financed by member countries, each contributing according to the size of its GDP.

OECD is subdivided into directorates that in turn are subdivided into divisions. One of the divisions is concerned expressly with 'education and training', its work being guided by an Education Committee (one of thirty or so OECD committees) consisting of representatives nominated by national ministries of education. In addition, there is a Centre for Educational Research and Innovation (CERI) that is funded out of a special budget to which each member country contributes; CERI is guided by a governing board consisting of educational experts nominated by each country.

The *World Bank*, which is affiliated to the United Nations, is composed of the International Bank for Reconstruction and Development (IBRD), set up in 1945, and the International Development Association (IDA), set up in 1960. Its main function is to supply loans for economic development and to provide technical assistance. It first began financing education in the early 1960s, mainly in recognition of the fact that economic growth was contingent upon the rate of educational development. Ultimate authority resides with the board of governors, one governor for each country, which meets once a year. Policies are implemented by a directing group of twenty executive directors. The Bank obtains its revenue from the subscriptions of member countries, flotations, and net earnings.

SIMILARITIES AND DIFFERENCES

Two outstanding common characteristics can be discerned. The first is that permanent secretariats play a preponderant role. In the CDCC and OECD a large proportion of the staff holds permanent appointments; in Unesco appointments are limited to two-year contracts but most of the staff are *de facto* employed indefinitely. The reality of permanence ensures that the secretariats not only execute each organization's policies but also frequently initiate them, even if by anonymous means. For this reason the quality of the output of each organization is largely determined by the

21

professional ability and zeal of its secretariat. Recruitment, retention, and career policies are therefore of capital importance. Second, the head of each organization exercises formidable powers. Juridically he is responsible in his person for all official actions: publications, for example, are issued in his name. He is in a position to set overall priorities. Subject to the necessity of observing either explicit or implicit national quotas for staff appointments, he can select senior officials. It follows that the thrust and reputation of the work of each organization reflect the convictions and administrative style of the top official. It also follows that whereas an organization will probably flourish under the leadership of a man of ideas who is dynamic and diplomatic, it will almost certainly founder under a weak or arbitrary or intellectually bankrupt leader.

As to differences, Unesco and the Bank nominally serve the whole world, whereas the CDCC and OECD serve a specific group of countries. For the CDCC, that means all the countries of western Europe, and for the OECD, all the countries of western Europe together with Australia, Canada, Japan, New Zealand, and the USA; Yugoslavia has the status of an associate member. The caveat regarding the world-wide remit of the first two is significant because, in reality, they serve the less developed countries (LDCs) rather than the advanced industrialized countries (AICs). The priorities of Unesco and the Bank are very largely predicated by the particular needs of the LDCs. For example Unesco has treated the combat against illiteracy as an imperative priority and the Bank has made non-formal, as opposed to formal, education an overriding concern.

Unesco and the Bank have active field programmes whereas the CDCC and OECD do not. But between the programmes of Unesco and the Bank there is a big difference in the scale and mode of financing. Unesco is chronically short of funds and its programmes tend to be organized in penny-packets and under-financed. By contrast the Bank offers substantial loans and its technical assistance projects, though rigorously costed, usually concern a major governmental initiative and are appropriately funded.

The formal degree of commitment to educational issues and problems varies from Unesco, for which it is absolute, through the CDCC, for which it is a high priority, to the Bank and OECD, for which it is a priority only in so far as it relates to economic as well as social development. At the same time, the formal nature of an organization's commitment has little to do with the quality of the

have been set up in Bangkok for Asia, in Dakar for Africa, in Cairo for the Arab States, and in Santiago for Latin America. These have proved to be effective in stimulating region-wide co-operation through meetings, conferences, publications, and joint projects. Today it can no longer be doubted that the educational influence and administrative efficiency of Unesco could be greatly increased if more powers and responsibilities were to be devolved to the regions and if the size of the headquarters staff were to be reduced.

Unesco has also sought to enrich certain of its activities by creating purpose-designed institutions, three of which have earned a solid reputation for the efficacy of their work: the International Institute for Educational Planning (Paris); the Institute for Lifelong Education (Hamburg); the International Bureau of Education (Geneva). Incidentally it might be argued that these institutions are successful precisely because, like the other three organizations under review, their aims and functions are clearly defined.

Although it is important for outside observers, especially those who are hostile critics, to recognize the limited resources at the disposal of international organizations, it does not follow that their financing should be on a much bigger scale. For if resources are too easily come by, experience shows that programmes get out of hand and administration becomes an end in itself. International educational needs are elastic and could absorb bottomless funds. Additional funds on a large scale could best be applied to setting up more organizations with specific aims and functions rather than financially reinforcing the existing ones. For it is more productive to have many lean, purpose-designed organizations than to have only a few large ones.

THE BALANCE SHEET

On education all four organizations hold liberal and enlightened views. They believe that it is everyone's birth-right, that it is the key not only to national but also to world-wide economic prosperity, not only to social cohesion within each country but also to international understanding and, in the case of Unesco, the preservation of world peace. These are not mere rhetorical sentiments, since they inform each organization's policies and programmes, even if seldom proclaimed. Thus the organizations have advocated the introduction of universal primary education, the extension of secondary education, wider public access to post-secondary education, equal opportunities for girls and women, and special facilities for the educational needs of minority groups and physically and mentally handicapped people. The very concentration of Unesco and the Bank on the less developed countries is sufficient testimony of their concern for social justice on a global scale.

The progressive stance towards education of the four organizations deserves stressing for it has meant that whatever the ideological debates and controversies taking place within countries the pressure from outside has favoured educational reforms in pursuit of egalitarian goals. Each might have assumed a more or less agnostic position, especially OECD and the Bank, given that their main *raison d'être* is to help promote economic growth. In practice, the organizations have helped reinforce progressive educational movements within countries. The fact that, today, everywhere in the world, the declared aims of education and the way in which education systems are structured are very similar is largely explained by the ecumenical philosophy of international organizations.

At the end of the day, however, the organizations must be judged by their positive results. This truism at once raises the problem that many of their activities are not amenable to anything like systematic measurement of inputs and outputs. The value of their activities as a group and the particular contribution of each one have to be approached largely subjectively.

All four generate and disseminate new ideas and concepts. Among these may be cited: lifelong learning, recurrent education, non-formal education, and functional literacy. The generation process is worth examining for its own sake. Just how are new ideas and concepts born? It would be an instructive research exercise to take any one of the four concepts cited and painstakingly to identify who, be it an individual or a group, first thought of it, how it was developed within an organization, and how it caught on internationally.

What frequently happens is that an individual staff member perceives the glimmer of an idea that is then elaborated with a few colleagues, and given more substantial shape, that is endorsed at the programme-development level, and that is put forward for exploration as part of the work programme. Thereafter the idea is investigated in depth until eventually a report is prepared. Whether the idea then takes off to become international currency depends on a variety of factors. What is beyond dispute is that from their conception, several ideas have spread throughout the world of education at astonishing speed. This is partly because many of those who represent countries on the governing bodies of international organizations are ever on the alert to promote at home any new idea or innovation that looks promising. At the same time, many professional educationists in universities and international associations as well as many of the officials running foundations are quick to latch on to any idea that comes across as novel and far-reaching in its implications. All four of the ideas cited above had even become post-graduate research topics within four to five years of being floated within international organizations. The typical sanctification of a new idea occurs when a professional journal devotes an entire issue to considering its various facets.

It is one thing for international organizations to propagate an idea that soon commands world-wide attention. It is quite another matter for such an idea to be translated into practical action by national education authorities. This gap explains at least some of the cynical judgements that are rendered. Not perceiving any or few concrete results, critics are inclined to accuse international organizations of peddling high-sounding but ultimately sterile ideas.

The charge of abstraction can scarcely be laid at the door of the Bank. Its programmes are addressed to concrete needs and in the main have concrete outcomes. For example having espoused the idea of non-formal education, the Bank has ensured that many of its grants are allocated expressly to utilitarian programmes such as the training of high-level technicians. Up to a point Unesco can also focus its technical assistance on specific programmes predicated by a specific idea such as functional literacy. However, the CDCC, the OECD, and Unesco, for most of what they do, cannot guarantee that an idea be translated into practice. What they have succeeded in doing, however, is to persuade a majority of member countries to welcome new ideas, if only in principle, or in the form of international declarations and conventions. For instance, *éducation permanente* for CDCC, recurrent education for OECD, and lifelong learning for Unesco.

Moreover, some countries have taken practical steps to act on a new idea. These are a minority, it is true, but a minority is surely better than no country reacting at all. Furthermore, a new idea may have a significant impact even when it is neither formally adopted by countries nor treated as a frame of reference for concrete reforms. For an innovatory spirit may be generated within countries directly as the result of a new idea being popularized by international organizations. Individual administrators, organizers, academics, inspectors, principals, teachers, and politicians are frequently moved to innovate as a result of attending an international meeting or reading an international report. The idea of lifelong learning, for example, may still not be reflected in the organization and practice of most national education systems, but it has undoubtedly greatly influenced the approach to their work of countless individuals concerned with education in all countries and at all levels.

Apart from generating new ideas, identifying emerging issues, and formulating key questions, international organizations collect, collate, and disseminate useful information on common problems and experiences. Individual researchers cannot hope to acquire comparative data across countries from official sources. Major research institutions can enjoy only limited success. The inter-governmental organizations, however, are in a position to collect information from their member countries on a significant scale and a regular basis. Their information-gathering is of two kinds:

1 that required for a specific enquiry into, say, multilingual education or the education of handicapped people, or non-traditional post-secondary education;
2 systematic basic statistics on educational trends and developments.

Information gathered for the purpose of carrying out specific programmes is of notable value. Thus Unesco has amassed a rich documentation on literacy and adult education. The Council of Europe has published numerous case studies on *éducation permanente*. The OECD has published case studies on, *inter alia*, the financing of education, recurrent education, and the education of handicapped people. The Bank has undertaken numerous analyses of national education and training policies and programmes, most of which, unfortunately, are confidential.

As to statistics, Unesco has been responsible for setting up and elaborating the International Standard Classification of Education Statistics (ISCED), which has become an indispensable source of information. The OECD has frequently published statistics on important aspects of education and has recently initiated an annual survey of comparative statistics on its member countries. In addition, international organizations contribute significantly to the dissemination of research findings. This is done by citing such findings in their reports and publications, and by issuing regular newsletters.

Despite all this, international organizations are often censured for an alleged failure to make their activities sufficiently widely known. The criticism is misplaced since it is not part of their formal duty to address a mass audience directly. They do ensure, however, that the responsible authorities in the member countries that they serve are suitably informed.

Unesco and the OECD publish many of their studies and reports commercially. Their circulation does not compare, however, with that of the leading international publishing houses, except for such a seminal book as *Learning To Be* (Unesco). But their publications are purchased by many general and specialized libraries, and by numerous departments and faculties of education.

OTHER ORGANIZATIONS

Many other organizations are concerned with the development of education by means of international discourse, exchanges, and field programmes. Some of the most effective, like the exchange and training sections of the EEC, are confined to specific geographic regions. The Nordic countries collaborate closely in the educational field. Several organizations, such as the International Labour Organization (ILO), concentrate on a particular branch of education. There exists, in addition, a host of non-governmental organizations, a few of which maintain important programmes. Collectively they cover almost every form of educational endeavour. All in all there is an extraordinary amount of international activity, far more, certainly, than is commonly realized. If its direct impact on educational practice is slight, its indirect impact should never be underestimated.

CONCLUSION

In the last resort any inter-governmental organization is only as effective as its member countries allow it to be. If they insist on tight control of all its programmes or withhold adequate resources, its performance is bound to disappoint. At the same time, some external control is essential, and internal checks and balances are

31

no less required. Nevertheless member countries that want satisfactory results must be prepared to leave an organization considerable freedom to innovate and to manage its own programme, and they must provide at least adequate funding.

The four organizations here reviewed, whatever their faults, continue to justify their existence. If they were to be abolished tomorrow there would doubtless soon be a move to replace them.

4

The International Council for Adult Education

Budd Hall

A group of people sat talking in a hotel room in the Prince Hotel in Tokyo, Japan, in 1972. After many years of working towards an international organization for the adult education movement, the time seemed right. The decision was taken to go ahead with the creation of the International Council for Adult Education (ICAE). The people were participants at the Unesco international conference on adult education, but the history of their efforts went back many years.

Today the ICAE functions as an international non-governmental organization, a voluntary and co-operative partnership of people and organizations working together for the education of adults for responsible, human-centred social and economic development. One of the men in the room of the Prince Hotel in Tokyo was the late J. Roby Kidd, a Canadian adult educator who provided the organizing energy to bring people together around the idea of a council for the movement. Helmuth Dolff of Germany, Arthur Stock of England, Paul Mhaiki of Tanzania, Paul Bertelsen of Denmark, Paul Lengrand of France, and Alex Charters of the USA were among the early team who helped put the network together. The initial push came from nineteen national and regional adult education associations, but the primary focus and strongest source of energy came from the Third World nations.

The founding honorary president was Julius K. Nyerere of Tanzania. Malcolm Adiseshiah of India, the former assistant director-general of Unesco, was the first president. J. Roby Kidd was the founding secretary-general. Dr Robert Gardiner of Ghana, former secretary of the Economic Commission of Africa, followed Dr Adiseshiah. The present president, Dame Nita Barrow of Barbados, has had a distinguished career in international voluntary service as former president of the World YWCA, the president for the Caribbean of World Council of Churches, as convenor of the 1985 NGO Forum for Women in Nairobi, and as member of the 1986 Commonwealth Eminent Persons Group to South Africa. A special characteristic of the ICAE is its regional and national adult education association membership. It is an international organization that provides support to member organizations and networks of activists rather than to individuals. There are at present ninety-two national, regional, and sectoral members from seventy-six nations and six regions of the world. Member organizations are expected to develop their own infrastructure, policy, and programmes. Each member is autonomous and self-reliant. Many of the members pre-date the existence of the International Council itself.

In addition to the national associations and regional association, a number of organizations hold sectoral membership in the council with full rights of participation. At present the sectoral members include the Nordic Folk High School Council, the Commonwealth Association for Adult Education and Training, the International Congress of University Adult Education, and the International League for Social Commitment in Adult Education. There are another thirty or so international non-governmental organizations, which are in a special relationship as 'Co-operating Organizations'. These include such varied bodies as ISIS, the major international women's network, the International Union of Students, the World Confederation of Organizations of the Teaching Profession, the International Federation of Library Associations, the Co-operative Alliance, and the International Council of Voluntary Associations.

The ICAE supports members and networks with information flow and dissemination, networking with other organizations, identifying resource people as required, identifying potential funders, providing learning and training opportunities for organizational staff, and assisting in the conceptualization of national and regional organization programming or projects when invited to do so.

Between 1984 and 1986 the ICAE sponsored or co-sponsored 51 meetings in 22 countries, attended by nearly 2,000 activists and leaders. Topics covered during this period included the following:

Secretaries of national associations
Role of international aid in adult education
Women and the microtech industry

Workers' education in Asia
Participatory research in many parts of the world
Literacy
Peace education
Co-operation with China
History of adult education

The Council publishes a quarterly journal, *Convergence*, a newsletter, specialized newsletters such as the women's programme, the participatory research network, the criminal justice newsletter, peace network, as well as reports from various conferences and events. These publications carry a wide variety of personal experiences, reports from local projects, calls to action, analytic articles, and generally reflect a dramatic picture of the vibrant and active nature of each movement.

One of the goals of the council, upon its creation, was to provide a voice for the adult education movement within the international inter-governmental systems. The council therefore maintains liaison status with the UN Economic and Social Commission, Unesco (A status), ILO (special list), FAO, Unicef, and the World Bank. It has named special representatives in Paris, Geneva, New York, and Ottawa in order to carry on this work.

STRUCTURE OF THE COUNCIL

General assembly

Each of the member associations has one vote in the general assembly. This body meets every four years to elect a new set of officers and to make the major decisions about the priorities of the organization. These world meetings have been held in Dar es Salaam, Tanzania, in 1976; in Helsinki, Finland, in 1979; in Paris in 1982; and in Buenos Aires, Argentina, in 1985.

Executive committee

An executive committee meets each year. At present it consists of thirty-three persons from twenty-nine different countries. The honorary president is Paulo Freire of Brazil. In addition to our president and secretary-general, there is a treasurer and a number

35

of vice-presidents, the latter nominated by the regional organizations. National associations nominate regional members to the executive, and all secretaries of regional organizations are automatic members. The executive is responsible for implementation of the policies of the ICAE and the monitoring of programmes and finances of the organization. They are aided in this by a series of committees: Management Advisory Committee, Programme Advisory Committee, Finance, International Relations, and Communications. Like the general assemblies, the executive meeting rotates each year. It has met in Trinidad, Shanghai, Moscow, Washington DC, Baghdad, and Montreal.

Secretariat

The secretariat is located in Toronto, Canada and consists of ten full-time persons. As an international and multilingual group, it is responsible for the day-to-day running of the council, for providing the ongoing support to the membership and networks, and for maintaining the basic communications infrastructure of the council.

Programme priorities

Programme priorities are set and monitored by the Programme Advisory Committee which reports to the executive and works directly with the president, the secretary-general, and the programme officers in the secretariat. As of February 1987, nine programmes have been designated as being of high priority, five as areas of special interest, and three as emerging areas. Special interest areas are those in which the ICAE might anticipate ongoing involvement, but they are not areas that would develop into large or full-fledged programmes. Emerging programmes require some special attention to help them develop their potential. These categories are reviewed each year and are open to new ideas.

Priority programmes
  Primary health care
  Women
  Training
  Literacy

Peace
Workers' education
Participatory research
Information
Convergence

Emerging programmes

Economic self-management
Education and criminal justice
New technology
Environment

Special interest areas

Education and older adults
History of adult education
Indigenous peoples
Disabled persons
Rural education

The J. Roby Kidd Fund

The J. Roby Kidd Fund was set up in 1982 after the death of Dr Kidd. Every year the fund recognizes the significant contribution of an adult educator to grassroots adult education: it seeks out innovative persons who have usually not been recognized previously for their efforts. The award is open to all adult educators.

The Nabila Breir Fund

A second fund was established in early 1987 in the memory of Ms Nabila Selback Breir of Lebanon, who was an active member of the ICAE's women's network and Programme Advisory Committee. She was killed in Beirut in December 1986 for her work in refugee camps in Southern Lebanon. The council is actively raising funds for this effort. The purpose of the fund will be to provide a chance for women adult educators from the Arabic-speaking world to be able to travel and meet with their sisters engaged in similar work in other parts of the world.

DE-CENTRALIZED NATURE OF PROGRAMMES

The ICAE works through its members and networks for all its work. It would be clearer to say that the ICAE *is* its members, networks, and their various activities. In principle, all of the programmes are

37

co-ordinated by people not located in Toronto. Although the programme may begin in Toronto, it is moved somewhere else when possible. For example the Participatory Research Network and the Workers' Education Network are co-ordinated from India. The Primary Health and Popular Education Network are co-ordinated from Santiago, Chile. Training is co-ordinated from the Caribbean, while History of Adult Education is co-ordinated from Norway.

This arrangement accomplishes several objectives:

1 It keeps the co-ordination of networks at a grassroots base, an action centre;
2 It builds centres of expertise around international dimensions of the areas of concern throughout the world;
3 It reduces tendencies towards dependency which sometimes arise in international work;
4 It provides many models of international co-operation which offer innovative possibilities rather than one 'formula' for running a network or programme.

Periodic evaluation

At least once every five years the ICAE initiates a thorough evaluation process which involves interviews, discussions, and questionnaires to all of various parts of the ICAE network. The most recent evaluation, completed by an independent outside team, was finished in February 1987. The results are being fed into all of the various committees, the members, and networks, and a process of review and discussion will be undertaken to set priorities for areas of action.

Some of the issues raised for future discussions are:

1 *Membership* Since the model of the ICAE membership was created in the early 1970s we have seen a growth of many thousands of non-governmental organizations springing up throughout the world. Many of these NGOs are adult education agencies working directly with local groups or with the public. Should these adult education organizations have a voice in the ICAE? This will be a discussion which will take some time.
2 *Language* How do we break the monopoly of English? English does not an international network make! Language is thought,

culture, and identity. The adult education movement more than most must find ways to communicate in at least French, Spanish, and Arabic. Within the regions many more languages are needed. But for voluntary under-resourced groups coping with the language question is a tough obstacle which needs much more work.

3 *Role of women* Getting women on the executive of the ICAE has been difficult. In spite of specific directives to member associations and positive reinforcement of organizations which have nominated women, there remains much to do. Women represent fewer than 30 per cent of the members of the current ICAE executive, and a much smaller percentage of national secretaries or directors. Men remain very much in control.

4 *Learning from our own work* How can an organization such as the council learn from its own work and the work of its members in a more systematic way? The ICAE has promoted the concept of participatory research in a substantial way, and yet currently has no research or evaluation capacity to examine the work that it is engaged in or supporting itself? How can some of the networks or research institutions of the international networks be tapped in order to stimulate this much-needed reflection? How can the ideas of popular educators at the base be systematized so that they can become the books which are read in the training sessions in our organizations?

5 *Increasing resources to the movement* There has been a tremendous growth in the number of national adult education associations over the years. The ICAE alone has grown from nineteen to ninety-two members in thirteen years. Adult education as a movement has matured and is capable of effectively utilizing much more money than is currently available. How can more resources be generated for the movement as a whole? Are there options for voluntary organizations other than government grants or foundation pleas? What forms of financial support can be found which do not carry explicit or implicit obligations to the directions of the funder?

CLOSING REMARKS

Peril and progress seem to be closer companions than ever these days. We are living in the midst of a global shift of resources, power, and perhaps even ideas. The decisions made in London,

Tokyo, New York, and Saudi Arabia affect our day-to-day life in minute and specific ways. The fabric of international financial coverage which has held more or less in place since the Second World War is frayed to tatters. Whole towns close down and people are put on the road from north to south, from rural to urban, from poor to rich, looking for work and too often looking for survival.

The networks of publications, media, classes, organizations, and community groups where we work give us as adult educators a place to hear the world in unique and constructive ways. We are beginning to have the structures to share what we are hearing on an international level. With support and encouragement and a little bit of luck we have the chance to build for ourselves an international movement which believes in people and their capacities for control and change. These are indeed dread and thrilling times.

5

Agencies for adult education in the Commonwealth

Alan Rogers

INTRODUCTION

This chapter is concerned with certain of the means for developing educational links and networks in the Commonwealth. Some of these are formal, some are non-formal in nature, and the balance between these is changing. In large part, the links are influenced by many of the changes in international co-operation which are taking place at the moment; but it may also be that the development of more effective educational links throughout the Commonwealth might itself influence various of these changes and help to create a stronger and more beneficial Commonwealth.

CHANGES IN COMMONWEALTH LINKS

When the Commonwealth countries, after the Heads of Government meeting in 1965, established in the Commonwealth Secretariat and in the regular Heads of Government and Commonwealth Ministers Meetings more formal machinery of co-operation at inter- governmental level, educational co-operation was not a major item on the agenda. Rather, the main concerns were in the fields of economic co-operation (especially development), mutual defence, and the preservation of internal stability to ensure effective political growth.

But as time has passed, things have changed in the balance of nations. Economic growth, for many Commonwealth countries, has come to rely more on the emergence of regional groupings of nations for economic co-operation, of which ASEAN and the EEC are only two examples. Similarly regional or local defence treaties have for many Commonwealth countries become more important than their earlier reliance on Britain and other Commonwealth powers. And of course many countries have deliberately pursued independent political policies rather than depend upon the constitutional inheritance from the earlier Empire or Dominions. So that in each of these fields, and in other respects, the Commonwealth links are less directly valued than they once were. Even in the field of international aid and development, the Commonwealth is less important than international bodies such as the World Bank and the various United Nations agencies; many developing countries of the Commonwealth look for more aid from organizations outside the Commonwealth than inside.

There has of course been a response within the Commonwealth to all of this. Some 'regions' have themselves emerged amongst Commonwealth countries: Australia and New Zealand for example with the South Pacific countries, especially the small island states; and Canada with the Caribbean states being but two examples of these groupings. But even these regional Commonwealth groupings are still for many Commonwealth countries not the most important of their international networks. And they have had one side-effect: to tend to isolate the United Kingdom from other parts of the Commonwealth even further than its own policies have done. The United Kingdom is not of course exempt from these general trends; it too has developed closer economic and defence links outside the Commonwealth with a regional group of nearer neighbours, the European Community. In relation to its Commonwealth links, it is true that in general the UK has been concentrating much of its efforts on Africa; but on the other hand, Africa has turned in many cases to the USA rather than to the UK for networking. Indeed the UK's persistent adherence to Europe since the early 1970s has been a sign of these changes and has also encouraged them.

Such tendencies have at times threatened the Commonwealth itself. Nevertheless, it has retained its sense of identity and its inter-governmental agencies through all the crises, especially those posed by the South African problem. Indeed at times, these very problems have provided a focus for joint decision-making and action which have helped to preserve and even strengthen the Commonwealth.

EDUCATION IN COMMONWEALTH LINKS

As these changes have taken place, there seems to have been something of an increase in the recognition of the centrality of educational matters as a foundation for Commonwealth relationships. Educational co-operation has become more important in the deliberations of the various governments that make up the Commonwealth. It features more frequently in discussions as defence and economic and political matters have become less prominent, and it is seen as one of the major means of strengthening Commonwealth bonds and of influencing other nations (for example, South Africa). We must not make too much of this trend; education is not of such major concern to many Commonwealth nations as for example 'development' or the nuclear issue; but nevertheless, some commentators have detected an increase in the profile given to educational matters as other matters have diminished in importance.

The reorganization of several of the different divisions within the Commonwealth Secretariat which contain elements of education and training in their programmes into a single 'Human Resource Development Group' (HRDG) may perhaps be seen as one sign of this new status. Nevertheless, 'education' *per se* is still a relatively minor matter of concern within the secretariat; the staff of the Education Division is only nine persons out of a total secretariat of some four hundred, or indeed twenty-six in the HRDG, and the educational budget is less than one-tenth of the total. But it seems to be clear that, compared with other topics of discussion, educational co-operation within the Commonwealth is increasing in importance, and the range of agencies and activities (though not apparently the resources) are increasing to match. Much of this of course is due to a growing perception that educational progress is related to 'development' in the Third World countries of the Commonwealth.

It should be noted here that this chapter is on the whole concerned with those agencies which are 'Commonwealth' in their status – although those national agencies which are involved in Commonwealth matters, such as the British government's ODA, the British Council, and so on, are themselves powerful agencies for co-operation within the Commonwealth. We are however here mainly discussing those agencies created and maintained jointly by the forty-nine countries and the thirteen territories which together make up the Commonwealth as a whole.

FACTORS FOR CO-OPERATION

Most discussions of Commonwealth co-operation stress those factors which tend to make it easy for the various partners to communicate and to combine together in joint programmes of action: factors such as a common language, similarities of tradition and of some aspects of political development (especially a common British civil service tradition), common professional development and ideals, and so on – what has been called 'a whole set of shared, and therefore "cementing", values and perceptions' (ICS, 1984: 2).

It is a moot point as to how far 'parallel educational systems [throughout the Commonwealth] had a large role in creating' these shared values and perceptions; but it is clear that these common factors are particularly strong in the field of education. The use in almost all Commonwealth countries of English in education at post-graduate level, which thus gives an impetus to the use of English at the lower levels of formal education, in the schools and colleges; the recognition in most Commonwealth countries of general and professional qualifications first established by Britain, however inappropriate some of these may now seem to be in the context of some developing countries; the work of London University in helping to establish university colleges in many Commonwealth countries (even to the extent of creating university extra-mural departments in the pattern of British universities, though in many parts of the Commonwealth, especially Africa, these were subsequently modified into institutes of adult education to meet more local needs); the inherited school curricula and patterns of teacher training, again despite their inappropriateness – all these have, so it is urged, made it possible for very diverse countries to talk to each other, to make visits and exchanges easy.

It is likely that these common factors are over-stressed, that the similarities are more imaginary than real. But that they are *felt* to exist at all is in itself significant; it provides a basis for discussion. Thus it is that recent challenges to educational co-operation, especially the unilateral decision by the United Kingdom on fees for overseas students in higher and advanced education courses, have generated such heat. How far the current desire in many countries for the 'diversification' of educational systems is a cause of or a response to widening gaps in all fields, including education, is not clear.

MEANS OF CO-OPERATION: OFFICIAL AND FORMAL

The main means of inter-governmental co-operation in the Commonwealth are the biennial meetings of the Heads of Government and the regular meetings of Commonwealth Ministers. Their meetings are prepared for them by, and they in turn set guidelines for the activities of, the Commonwealth Secretariat staff.

The objectives set for the Commonwealth Secretariat are to promote consultation and co-operation between all Commonwealth member states, and to help forward the development of the developing countries of the Commonwealth. There is in addition some outreach beyond the Commonwealth: some heads of government see the Commonwealth as a force in the world at large (the work with Namibian refugees and the impact of the Commonwealth on the apartheid problem are two instances of this). But the main subjects of discussion relate to matters of common interest to 'the club members' themselves. The Commonwealth Heads of Government, in their meetings, set the overall targets (such as the recent decision to give priority to the needs of small island states in the Commonwealth), and the regular meetings of the particular ministers, within those policy guidelines, establish the programmes for the different sections of the secretariat.

The Education Programme (which is now part of the Human Resource Development Group in the Commonwealth Secretariat) was established in 1966. It succeeded the earlier Commonwealth Education Liaison Unit which in turn had been set up in 1960 following the first meeting of the Commonwealth ministers of education in 1959. Its main aim is to help the Commonwealth member states to develop their individual educational and training systems according to their own policies, and to carry out the specific mandates entrusted to them by the Commonwealth heads of government and ministers of education in their respective meetings. The Programme thus promotes co-operation between Commonwealth countries, keeps educational developments under review, acts as a centre of reference for information, and promotes the study of specific topics of educational interest by research and publications. This division of the Commonwealth Secretariat works primarily through conferences, seminars, workshops, and training courses, either international or regional. It prepares or commissions and publishes reports and specialist studies, surveys, and handbooks; it provides and shares information, especially through

Commonwealth Education News, which it issues three times a year; it also provides some consultancies for individual member states.

The activities of the Education Programme of the Commonwealth Secretariat are guided (under the policies established by the meetings of ministers) by the Commonwealth Education Liaison Committee, a London-based committee established in 1959 and comprising representatives of each of the Commonwealth High Commissions in London, together with a few other bodies such as the Commonwealth Foundation and the Association of Commonwealth Universities. The main areas of current concern which have operated for the last few years include a number of controversial topics, especially the question of higher education fees and student mobility in the Commonwealth which has occupied the minds of many people throughout the Commonwealth since 1980; indeed, the question of the exchange of students in higher education and professional training has been one of the key areas of Commonwealth co-operation from very early days and remains an important element in the Secretariat's discussions today. Other topics are less controversial: higher education staff development and institutional linkages, for example; these have become more important as student exchange has become more difficult.

The Secretariat as a whole retains a direct interest in such matters: thus the Secretariat has a standing committee on student mobility which keeps such matters as the comparability of programmes and student finances constantly under review; a series of influential reports has appeared on these issues. Another such general matter under discussion at the moment is distance education (seen by many in the Commonwealth to be synonymous with open learning) and the possibility/desirability of establishing a Commonwealth Open University, the theme of a recent speech by the secretary-general of the Commonwealth Secretariat; a working party on Commonwealth co-operation in distance education was established in November 1986 and presented its report to be considered by the Commonwealth ministers of education at Nairobi in July 1987, suggesting that co-operation in this direction should be diversified rather than made more uniform.

Some of the issues which occupy the Secretariat's Education Programme are determined by the political and financial priorities of the member states. Thus for instance the question of resources for education (especially financial resources) seems to feature prominently in many parts of the programme; concern with total expenditure on formal education and the resources available, particularly in many of the poorer countries with rapidly increasing populations; cost-effective approaches to the primary and secondary curriculum and to the teaching of practical subjects (for example low-cost equipment for science and technical education); the costs of small schools; student loan schemes and the possibility of community funding for schools, and the use of schools as local community development centres. But other issues of current educational orthodoxy also appear: the question of the relevance of schooling to employment, including school-to-work transition and post-school technical training; and the application of new technology to school, higher, and non-formal education, both through the use of satellites and micro-computers in schools. The problems of creating adequate structures for education in small island states is one of the themes of the current programme, and there is a small but recurring interest in teaching and learning about the Commonwealth itself. These areas are not seen as entirely discrete items on the agenda of the Education Programme of the Secretariat; rather they are general fields of activity which in many cases overlap.

Clearly, with a small staff and minimal finances, not all of these topics can be covered at the same level all the time. There are signs that the resources of the Programme are over-stretched. Priorities are therefore essential, and these are set by the ministers of education in their regular meetings and with the advice of the CELC.

It is important to stress that (as a former head of the then Education Division put it) the Secretariat is the servant of forty-nine member governments, so that 'we should not look to the Secretariat *per se* for innovations or decision-making'. The Education Programme thus is primarily a responsive and consultative body rather than an initiating and directive one. And it is inter-governmental, not easily relating to the voluntary sector (except in the non-formal education programmes which the Commonwealth education ministers have mandated to them), though there is some activity in conjunction with NGOs, especially the Commonwealth Professional Associations.

There are other programmes within the Human Resource Development Group which include some education and training amongst their activities. Amongst these are the Health Programme, the Fellowships and Training Programme, the Management

Development Programme, the Women and Development Programme, and the Commonwealth Youth Programme. These are perhaps concerned with the more non-formal and continuing education aspects of co-operation rather than with formal educational systems. And of course training forms part of the interests of other parts (such as the Food Production and Rural Development Division, the International Affairs Division, and the Economic Affairs Division) of the Commonwealth Secretariat.

One of the biggest programmes within the Secretariat lies with the Commonwealth Fund for Technical Co-operation (CFTC). Established in 1971, it has been described as 'the development arm of the Secretariat'. It has enjoyed a relatively large – and until recently in some areas at least growing – budget. Its main work is to provide what is usually called 'technical assistance' rather than education, and it does this through the provision of 'experts' and through the development of training programmes for developing countries in the Commonwealth. On the whole it prefers to operate on a 'south–south' rather than a 'north–south' mode of linkage. The exchange of personnel, the funding of attendance at training programmes in another Commonwealth country, attachments, and study visits all form part of the activities of this section of the secretariat and of its Industrial Development Unit.

At the higher education level, the bilateral exchange of students in courses (mostly post-graduate courses) is supported by the Commonwealth Scholarship and Fellowship Programme which was established as early as 1960.

COMMONWEALTH FOUNDATION

The second major Commonwealth agency is the Commonwealth Foundation. Established in 1965 to 'administer a fund for increasing interchanges between Commonwealth organizations in professional fields' (Johnson, T.J. and Caygill, M., p.250; see ICS 1984: 37–9), and funded directly by Commonwealth governments, its relative independence makes it able both to take initiatives and to relate to the non-governmental sector more easily than the Secretariat.

The primary aim of the foundation is to strengthen the bonds between the Commonwealth countries; its areas of interest now include the arts and culture as well as professional education and training. But the majority of its work is still with professional organizations. It seeks to encourage and support the organization of and attendance by Commonwealth bodies and individuals at professional conferences; to help exchanges of professionals, and to promote the flow of professional information around the Commonwealth.

It is willing to assist in the setting up of national or regional professional bodies in countries where they do not at present exist; and by the promotion of Commonwealth-wide or regional associations, it hopes to reduce the centralization of Commonwealth bodies in Britain.

But the Foundation's work is not exclusively directed towards professional co-operation: it assists associations and ndividuals whose activities lie outside the strictly professional field but which encourage inter-Commonwealth exchange and development in the less developed countries of the Commonwealth. And it is not tied to multilateral inter-governmental co-operation. It has for instance recently launched an ambitious programme to establish Local Liaison Units for NGOs in various regions of the Commonwealth; so far such units have been discussed for the South Pacific, parts of Asia, and the Caribbean. Awards and grants are made for exchanges, visits, short-term fellowships, and other activities which have an inter-Commonwealth element in their programme; prizes are given in some fields such as literature.

CPAs

The largest of the Foundation's programmes relates to the establishment or support of Commonwealth Professional Associations (CPAs). Building on the informal networks which had sprung up in the early days of the Commonwealth and seeking to preserve and indeed to enhance these networks, the Foundation has assisted the older bodies and promoted the establishment of new associations in several areas.

There are currently some thirty-one of these, several of them wholly independent of Foundation funding but recognized and supported in other ways; others are more heavily dependent upon the Foundation. These associations link together practitioners in the various disciplines throughout the Commonwealth, and seek to promote status and standards and particularly to direct their resources towards the development of the less developed populations of the Commonwealth. There are thus associations for broadcasters, librarians, archivists, journalists, magistrates, nurses,

49

architects, engineers, surveyors and planners, lawyers, and so on. Some link together individual practitioners, others national professional bodies in the various Commonwealth countries, and some promote the establishment of national or regional bodies where these do not already exist. There are some who see the role of such professional associations as diminishing with the decline of the Anglo-centric view of the Commonwealth and indeed with the growth of what might be called multi-centric concepts of the professions, as each of the member states works out for themselves precisely what a particular profession means for them in the light of their own experience, resources, and needs. Nevertheless, the CPAs still exist and continue to flourish, more it seems from demand from the field than from persuasion from the centre.

Almost all of these Commonwealth Professional Associations have co-operation in the field of education and training as one of their major objectives. Several, such as the Commonwealth Nurses Federation, devote much time to the programmes of initial training in formal institutions; some, like the Commonwealth Human Ecology Council, seek to promote a particular field of study in formal and non-formal education alike. Others are more concerned with ongoing training for practitioners (what is called in some professions 'in-service' or 'continuing' education). Training courses for various regions of the Commonwealth are promoted and supported through the CPAs; trainers are sent from one Commonwealth country to another. But the major emphasis of most of the CPAs has been and still is 'on such questions as standards, uniformity and reciprocal recognition'. The debate as to whether the creation of 'a Commonwealth community of professional [with the successful] imposition of uniform standards [would] prove as advantageous for the developing countries of the Commonwealth as the community of professionals argue it would' (Johnson, T.J. and Caygill, M., 1972: 273), which was strong in the early 1970s, is still relevant today, even though the professionals from the developing countries are now more fully involved in the determination of those 'uniform standards'.

Several of the CPAs are more specifically educational in their nature. The Commonwealth Legal Education Association for example is concerned with legal training courses rather than the practice of law. The Association of Commonwealth Universities is in a category of its own. With its own premises and staff and its large programme of staff interchange between Commonwealth universities and its publications, it is unlike most of the CPAs, in that it is responsive rather than initiatory. To some extent it relies upon the support of the various governments for its programmes, and its concerns are with the whole Commonwealth, however much it may wish to direct resources towards the developing areas of the Commonwealth. The Commonwealth Council for Education Administration (CCEA) draws together administrators in the formal sectors from school to university; it has a membership of some 3,300 through national associations or individuals. Its headquarters are housed in the Faculty of Education of the University of New England in Armidale, Australia, for whom the executive director of the association works in a part-time capacity. CASTME (the Commonwealth Association of Science, Technology, and Mathematics Educators) has a membership of about 200; it is concerned to promote the social significance of science, technical, and mathematics education, science education in schools and throughout the population at large, to encourage scientific understanding and attitudes in the Commonwealth, and to direct scientific resources towards developmental problems. It publishes a newsletter and provides an award scheme to encourage innovations in science, technical, and mathematics teaching; its Secretariat is based at the Commonwealth Secretariat.

The most recent of these professional associations is the Commonwealth Association for the Education and Training of Adults (CAETA). This body was founded – after some hesitation on the part of the foundation – as a response to considerable pressure from a number of sources: Commonwealth adult educators gathered in international assemblies in Delhi (1979), Paris (1982), and elsewhere; some of the other CPAs; and the Commonwealth Foundation Symposium in Barbados in 1982. In 1984 the Commonwealth Foundation agreed that a small London(UK)-based informal committee should be assisted to invite Edward Ulzen of the African Association for Literacy and Adult Education to undertake a feasibility study, and later that year the Foundation's board accepted his recommendation that such an association should be formed, and made an initial grant for this purpose. There was some delay before the association was finally launched, but from its active inception early in 1986, CAETA has grown, clearly responding to a felt need throughout many parts of the Commonwealth. By the middle of 1987 membership numbered more than 600.

From the start, CAETA has sought to draw together individuals in Commonwealth countries who are engaged in all forms of

51

education and training for adults – especially those outside the traditional adult education areas such as community workers, industrial trainers, and extension workers – and to promote the educational aspect of their work. The fact that in all countries of the Commonwealth adult education and continuing education are not covered by statutory provisions, that no formal training programmes are provided for the education and training of adults, and that no formal qualifications are required before anyone may teach adults means that there is a considerable sense of need for professional development on the part of many practitioners in this field. And the non-formal and unstructured nature of post-school educational provision means that the practitioners of education and training for adults in Commonwealth countries – especially in the developing countries – work in a wide variety of agencies and often feel isolated from each other. The association thus seeks to work with national and regional bodies in adult education and extension in developing locally based and ongoing programmes of professional development for all those who are engaged in teaching adults.

The association is deeply involved in developmental programmes. It thus works not only with formal adult education bodies but also with a range of voluntary development agencies and with many non-educational government bodies – ministries of labour or health or agriculture, for example. Further, CAETA seeks to encourage such attitudes amongst adult educators in the more developed countries of the Commonwealth. The association publishes a newsletter, and plans to develop networks of similarly interested practitioners, organize and promote exchanges, visits, and study tours, and provide Commonwealth-wide and regional workshops on aspects of training and resource development.

The inauguration of the association provides an example of the thinking which underlies the work of this body. Held in a rural area of India in March 1987, it took the form of a training workshop in resource identification and exploitation. A two-day study tour of adult education in the slums of Bombay was followed by two days of field-work with rural programmes and an intensive three-day group programme writing a report. The inaugural workshop was attended by 104 members of the association from 31 countries.

The policy of the association is to strengthen as far as possible the professional development programmes of the various countries and regions of the Commonwealth, but it also plans to conduct 'training the trainers' courses in various regions, to promote research programmes, to provide information and consultancy services, and to publish studies as part of the association's future programme as a professional association for its members. It has an interim office at the University of Reading School of Education with a part-time honorary secretary-general and some typing assistance; permanent arrangements will be made by the newly elected executive council.

Educational co-operation then in the Commonwealth is not solely, nor perhaps even primarily, a matter for inter-governmental activity; it is also undertaken by a number of voluntary non-governmental bodies. Such co-operation is of course as much at a personal as at an institutional level; as with most forms of post-formal education, it is very disjointed. There is some concern to promote co-operation between the various CPAs. The Commonwealth Foundation sought to draw together the members of different CPAs in various regions by setting up a number of Commonwealth Professional Centres in different regions; so far nine have been established. CAETA has expressed a desire to work with other CPAs in their training programmes, particularly through a 'training of trainers for the professions' course; and more recently, responding to a proposal from CAETA, the Commonwealth Secretariat Education Programme has discussed with three of the more specifically educational CPAs ways of linking their work with its own programmes.

OTHER LINKAGES

There are several other forms of educational co-operation and linkage within the Commonwealth. The most important must still be the UK examining boards, though the influence of these is steadily declining. The Royal Commonwealth Society, based in its headquarters and with its unique library in London (UK) and branches elsewhere, promotes a variety of activities leading to greater understanding of and concern for the Commonwealth, and there are similar societies in India, Canada, and elsewhere. The Commonwealth Association of Polytechnics in Africa draws together many technical training establishments in that continent. The Council for Education in the Commonwealth in Britain is a parliamentary-based body which provides a forum for discussion of British participation in Commonwealth educational development, mostly at school and college level.

Several other bodies such as the Commonwealth Institute (supported both by the British government and the various Commonwealth High Commissions in London) and independent bodies such as the University of London's Institute of Commonwealth Studies (often in collaboration with the Department of International and Comparative Education in that university's Institute of Education) serve an important Commonwealth educational function.

And finally it has been pointed out that many other bodies throughout the Commonwealth – many of them in the UK – ranging from the Bank of England to the Church of England, from the British Library to Parliament and the armed forces, from the many scientific societies to the BBC, from cricket to the press and the broadcasting agencies, have all developed and cherish Commonwealth-wide linkages, many of them involving educational and training aspects. It has been well and often commented that the value [of these links] is out of all proportion to the resources involved.

FUTURE TRENDS

It is perhaps hazardous to guess at future trends in educational co-operation in the Commonwealth. There are after all many uncertainties built into the Commonwealth itself, and although most commentators are on the whole optimistic, political events like the recent clash over sanctions on South Africa could ultimately weaken and finally dissolve the whole body (though this is unlikely). It is not at all clear whether the so-called 'cement' on which the Commonwealth – and these Commonwealth linkages – are founded is real or only apparent, or indeed whether these very linkages (especially some of the more influential ones such as the ACU) themselves create and maintain the Commonwealth and thus hold these very disparate nations together. But there are still those who hope that the style of co-operation developed so painfully over the years since 1947 'can overcome self-sufficiency aspirations and dependency fears while at the same time showing that diversification works best when language and legacies are shared'.

Within the field of educational co-operation and the agencies which contribute to it, however, we can note one or two current trends which point the way towards the future. First, education in the Commonwealth suffers from an attitude on the part of many government and non-government aid agencies which emphasizes its instrumental (training) nature rather than any other. Indeed, several such bodies indicate firmly that they 'do not fund education, only training', a factor which distorts some co-operative programmes. One expression of this strongly instrumental attitude towards training and away from a wider concept of education is a reluctance on the part of some Commonwealth bodies to strengthen multilateral links in the Commonwealth and to concentrate instead on bilateral programmes. Britain – and to a lesser extent Australia – are amongst those countries who prefer Commonwealth co-operation (in education as in other matters) to be on a country-to-country basis. The suggestion for a 'Commonwealth Open University' under discussion in 1987 is a good example of this. Some countries wish to extend existing distance learning resources throughout the Commonwealth by making individual agreements; others wish to establish a central (though in this case small) centre to foster, promote, and even on occasion to initiate multilateral co-operation. This tension lies at the heart of today's Commonwealth.

Second, there is an apparent movement towards the non-formal rather than increasing the formal, especially in many of the developing countries. There is still a great demand for co-operation in the formal sectors, especially at the higher and advanced educational level, as each member state develops its own higher education system to meet its own needs and national development goals. But the problems of paying for university education and of universalizing primary education in many countries with financial problems and/or rapid population growth (a growth which calls for ever-expanding expenditure on higher education as well as on primary educational facilities) have caused many governments to look towards the non-formal and adult sectors. The 'Commonwealth Non-formal Education for Development' conference, held in Delhi in 1979, and its follow-up on evaluation in non-formal education in Dhaka in 1984 are one sign of this; more recently workshops have been held in Zimbabwe (on alternative patterns of post-primary education), Malawi (on the use of rural schools as rural community resource centres intended for development as well as educational provision), and London (on distance learning), all signs of this developing focus.

It is significant that several of the staff of the Commonwealth Secretariat Education Programme have considerable experience in the non-formal education sectors. Members of the team are drawn from many Commonwealth countries such as Kenya, Malaysia, New Zealand, and Ghana, and their expertise and interests are very varied. But in this the alternative fields of educational enterprise feature prominently. The director, Peter Williams, was part of the Unesco team which included people such as Asher Deleon and Paul Lengrand, both noted for their approaches to lifelong learning rather than formal initial education; this group served as the Secretariat for the International Commission on the Development of Education, which under the guidance of Edgar Faure of Canada produced the report *Learning To Be* (1973), a major event in the world of non-formal education, influencing as it has the thinking of educationalists in Third World countries though less influential amongst educationalists in the economically more developed countries of the Commonwealth. Again, Dr Hilary Perraton's involvement in distance learning is well known, and his experience adds to the strength of the Education Programme's expertise in this area. The impetus towards the non-formal within the Secretariat's Education Programme is thus considerable and reflects the growing interest throughout the Commonwealth in these aspects of educational provision.

But while there are undoubted trends in the direction of increasing both non-formal structures and non-formal methods of educational provision, equally there are those who, in their concern to achieve wider, more effective, and less expensive initial education for all young people in their countries, view non-formal education as simply an extension of the formal systems to reach audiences as yet untouched – a part-time, and therefore cheaper, version of primary schooling. 'Adult education' is not popular in many countries of the Commonwealth today, and there are signs of impatience at the inability of adult and non-formal agencies to 'deliver the goods'. It is therefore likely that as the debate continues, the formal will influence the non-formal more than vice versa. In these circumstances the emergence of CAETA with its stress on non-formal and developmental out-of-school education could be important.

Acknowledgements

Through the generosity of many people, I have been able to consult and quote from a number of papers (some of them unpublished) relating to the programmes of the bodies mentioned in this chapter.

Among those who have assisted in the provision of material are Miss Margaret Beard of the University of London's Institute of Commonwealth Studies and Peter Williams of the Commonwealth Secretariat. Several people have read early drafts of this paper, including Peter Williams and John Macpherson, Maurice Goldsmith, Kenneth King, Edwin Townsend Coles, and Professor Paul Fordham, and I am grateful for the comments I have received. It must however be stressed that the comments contained within this paper are mine and do not necessarily reflect the views of any others.

REFERENCES

The following published reports have been useful in preparing this chapter:

Johnson, T.J. and Caygill, M. (1972) *Community in the Making: Aspects of Britain's Role in the Development of Professional Education in the Commonwealth*, University of London Institute of Commonwealth Studies.

Morris-Jones, W.H. (ed.) (1984) *The Commonwealth as an Educational Network: Trends and Problems*, report of seminar, University of London Institute of Commonwealth Studies.

Part 3

Regional organizations

6

The African Adult Education Association

Edward Ulzen

HISTORICAL BACKGROUND

The concept of adult education in its broadest sense and as defined by the Unesco General Conference held in Nairobi, Kenya (1976) is not new to Africa. Long before the period of colonialism, adult or community education was the means through which traditions, that is the body of principles and experiences that governed the African societies in their growth and development, were transmitted through generations. The traditional adult/community education also enabled the 'equipping of the individual with the basic skills necessary for life with those qualities and values that would make him acceptable to society' (Wandira 1971). The objectives of the traditional adult education were very clear and

> its work involved the family, the individual members of society in inculcating in youth and adults the norms, habits and attitudes which were essential to a peaceful and smooth existence of the society . . . : the adult was also trained in agriculture and handicraft which were aimed to provide him with the means of existence in life . . . and was introduced to subjects like religion and politics so that he could have a proper understanding of society and thus be able to adapt himself to the changes constantly taking place.
>
> (Okedara and Stanford 1974)

The important elements in the traditional adult/community education were the acquisition of community awareness, the learning of accepted values and culture, the absorption of the general stock of knowledge, training of leaders, and the acquisition of skills economically useful to society.

(Bown and Olu Tomori 1979)

The traditional adult education lost its importance and place during the period of colonialism when rulers put the premium on formal and 'school' education to the exclusion of adult education to meet the bureaucratic and administrative exigencies of their governments.

On the eve of the independence of most African countries, especially those under British rule, there already existed a number of national bodies in adult education such as the People's Education Association in the Gold Coast (now Ghana), Sebenta in Swaziland, and the Workers' Educational Association in Sudan during the late 1940s. It was in early 1954, however, that the first step towards achieving an international organization or forum for adult education was taken in the convening of a conference on 'Adult Education in a Changing Africa' by the then Institute of Extra-Mural Studies of the University College of the Gold Coast (Ghana) and the International Federation of Workers' Education Associations in Legon, Ghana, which brought together adult educators from West and East Africa and Sudan. This was the first gathering of people interested in the development of a voluntary organization in adult education as opposed to people concerned with government programmes. In early 1960 another step was taken again in Ghana towards the formation of an inter-African organization of university adult educators in a meeting of adult educators from universities in North America and Africa.

On the other side of the continent, a series of periodic conferences of adult educators, revolving around the Institutes of Extra-Mural Studies of the Colleges of the University of East Africa, consisting of Kenya, Tanzania, and Uganda, was taking place. These conferences culminated in a conference on Residential Adult Education held in Kivukoni College, Tanzania, in 1964, where the idea of a Pan-African Association was discussed. This was followed by the formation of an Adult Education Association of East and Central Africa during a meeting on Adult Education and the Mass Media held at the Evelyn Home College of Further Education in Zambia in 1965. The association's activities soon aroused the interest of people outside its geographical area and at the association's annual conference held in Makerere University College, Kampala, in Uganda, attended by adult educators from seven countries including observers from Ghana and Sudan, the African Adult Education Association was created on 4 January 1968.

OBJECTIVES

The main objectives of the association were

1 to promote adult education in all forms in Africa and particularly by encouraging the formation of national adult education associations in member countries;
2 to arrange objective study of and research into the problems of adult education in contemporary Africa by all appropriate means, including conferences, seminars, study groups, and exhibitions;
3 to act as a clearing-house for information on all forms of adult education relating to Africa;
4 to publish reports of the educational activities and special studies of the association and similar bodies;
5 to publish and encourage publication or production of books, journals, pamphlets, and visual and other materials contributing to the purposes of the association;
6 to institute, confer, and award fellowships, scholarships, bursaries, medals and prizes, and other distinctions and awards;
7 to encourage affiliated national associations to arrange conferences, courses, lectures, study groups, seminars, and exhibitions on subjects affecting the citizen;
8 to co-operate with any society, association, or body, private or public, in any matters which will be conducive to the attainment of the association's objectives.

For the purposes of examining how and whether the association strove to achieve these main and ultimate objectives, the period of the existence of the association can be delineated into three phases. Each of these phases related to the periodic Unesco World Conferences on Adult Education and meant the assumption of immediate and specific but shifting objectives by the association in its attempts to reach the long-term and ultimate objectives. The development of adult education thought in Africa has had over the years substantial in-puts from a number of Unesco conferences: the Montreal Conference (1960), through Tokyo Unesco General

Conference (1972), the Nairobi Unesco General Conference (1976), and lastly the Unesco International Conference on Adult Education, Paris (1985). The process of the development of adult education thought in Africa has, in its turn, influenced the assumption of shifting objectives of the association in the efforts to attain its ultimate objectives.

THE FORMATIVE YEARS: 1968 TO 1976

The formation of the association occurred after the Montreal Conference (1960) when, as stated earlier, the struggle of independence had gripped the attention of the local 'political' leaders in African colonies. The struggle for independence had been either instigated or reinforced by the numerous demobilized soldiers who had fought in India and Burma, and who could not understand these countries' early attainment of independence while their countries still remained colonies. These adults pressed for more out-of-school education and accelerated the struggle for independence. The achievement of political independence by most African countries immediately led to the political search across frontiers and linguistic barriers, which culminated in the creation of the Organization of African Unity (OAU) in 1963 aimed at consolidating the national independence achieved; at coalescing the energies of the African countries in order to enable Africans to have a voice in the world; and at the creation of a sense of regional identity. The creation of the OAU had created a sense of regional identity for Africa in the political sphere, from which spawned numerous movements for similar Pan-African organizations across national boundaries and linguistic barriers in the social, economic, and cultural spheres. The Montreal Conference in 1960 had also established the fact of adult education being another professional system of education *vis-à-vis* the formal education system, and had indicated to the governments of the newly independent countries, the majority of whose citizens had not had the benefit of formal education, the potential in these adults which could be harnessed and enhanced into suitable manpower for national development. The spirit of regionalism and the Montreal Conference accelerated the search for a Pan-African organization in adult education which was being made in both East and West Africa into the formation of the African Adult Education Association (AAEA).

The main pre-occupation of the association during this period was in three main areas: advocacy; identification and pooling together of resources; and the struggle for the acceptance of adult education as a discipline in universities and as a profession in the public service. First, the association was dominated by university professors and teachers and a few practitioners in the field, who were engaged in mass campaigns and community and adult education programmes initiated by their governments. The work of advocacy with governments and political leaders was assumed by these persons in the institutes of extra-mural studies of universities, who had the funds and were then more able than others to travel around to conferences and seminars in Africa to meet with colleagues and to discharge this responsibility in the course of their own university work. They also possessed the philosophical knowledge, the professional know-how, and the foresight, greater than any other persons at the time, to see the need for the formation of a Pan-African Organization and to nurture its growth. Institutes in the universities of Ghana, East Africa, Ethiopia, Sudan, Zambia, and Nigeria shouldered this responsibility for advocacy, gained the recognition of their governments, as evidenced in the increased funding for their programmes, and spearheaded the formation and/or promotion of national associations.

Second, the association, through the professors and lecturers in university adult education institutions and the few practitioners in the field, began to identify the human and material resources within their countries and in other countries, which could be harnessed and utilized for adult education programmes and for the promotion and expansion of the movement in Africa. A core of professionals and practitioners was established, therefore, through whose discussions and work the development of adult education and its practices within the authentic African social and cultural context and with traditional antecedents was being achieved.

Third, as the result of the Montreal Conference, which established adult education as a profession, university adult education institutions graduated from short-term residential courses provided to workers in adult education to certificate, diploma, and degree courses, approved by the senates of the universities. Adult education by the early 1970s had been accepted by African universities as a discipline in its own right within their study programmes and was being accorded its rightful place by African governments.

THE GROWTH YEARS: 1977 TO 1982

This period occurred after three important conferences: the Third Unesco World Conference in Adult Education in Tokyo (1972), the Nineteenth Unesco General Conference in Nairobi (1976), and the Third General Assembly of the International Council for Adult Education in Dar es Salaam (1976). The Third Unesco World Conference in Adult Education, attended by the governments of all former colonies in Africa, excepting the Portuguese colonies, confirmed the importance of adult education as an essential ingredient in the socio-economic development of African countries. The Nineteenth Unesco General Conference adopted the recommendations on the development of adult education, which, *inter alia*, urged each member state to recognize adult education as a necessary and specific component of its education system and as a permanent element in its social, cultural, and economic development policy (Unesco Nineteenth General Conference Report 1976). The Third General Assembly of the International Council for Adult Education held in Africa for the first time provided a potent and fresh fillip to the African Adult Education Association.

The establishment of the association's secretariat in 1976, with the support of the International Council for Adult Education and funding by the Canadian International Development Agency, occurred within the context of a region, the attention of whose governments and people had been focused on adult education. The secretariat immediately planned to promote the formation of national associations of its members throughout sub-Saharan Africa; to bring the knowledge of its existence, objectives, and programmes to all African governments and organizations; to develop training programmes for regional and sub-regional workshops involving practitioners and middle-level adult education workers; to create networks of communication between agencies, trainers, and practitioners; and to undertake studies and research in adult education and publish their results as well as provide a forum for exchange of information.

The association had to determine the means through which it would realize its objectives without interfering with or inhibiting the freedom of its national association members in developing their own policies and realizing them in regard to their own objectives, programmes, and activities within the context of contributing to the attainment of their national development plans. Its efforts, therefore, were aimed at helping in the training of its members in order to reach a respectable professional status; and in undertaking programmes in various countries, to bring the aims, objectives, and activities to the notice and for participation of governments; and through these means create a virile, respectable, and continent-wide professional body at the disposal of governments and interested organizations. With a clientele embracing academicians, full-time practitioners, volunteer teachers, and organizers, it was clear that the association should exercise circumspection and discretion in formulating its programmes. Other considerations demanded caution: the association had no country but a continent, a fact which made its task multifold; the human and material resources available to the association were limited; the permanent staff at the secretariat was a bare-bone outfit; and there were numerous universities and other institutions in a number of countries able to provide training at some or all levels to their nationals. The association had at the same time to operate within nations, which were not always sure or firm in what they wanted in terms of ideology, thus inhibiting the apolitical nature of programmes of the association.

The association, in the circumstances, determined that its training instruments should consist of conferences, seminars, workshops, publications (including the newsletter and journal), and documentation. The main instrument was to be the training workshops. The programmes for each biennial meeting, previously discerned by the secretariat through visits and correspondence, were determined during the biennial conferences by the members. The training needs of each programme were furnished by the national associations and harmonized so as to be relevant to the sub-regions and the region. These workshops brought together adult educators and practitioners from various backgrounds and countries and provided a forum for the cross-fertilization of ideas, experiences, practices, and information in adult and non-formal education and the realization that each association and member was a part of a wider adult education movement. They provided a forum for the establishment and strengthening of personal and official communication between the national associations and the AAEA as well as between the participants, the latter facilitating and advancing mutual action and support for adult education programmes. The workshops, further, provided a period for 'doers' and practitioners, a period for theoretical reflection and academic insights to their work, and introduced them to academic and theoretical sources of knowledge. Finally, these workshops were meant to be both catalytic and cathartic, so as to enable participants as well as their national associations to replicate them in their countries with modifications appropriate to their circumstances and special needs.

The secretariat, set up to spearhead these activities, in consequence of the lack of human and financial resources, did not attempt to establish itself as 'a centre-to-periphery structure, with a fixed centre and a clearly defined leadership', in which 'the communication is from centre to outward and the messages are stable, requiring simply the application of a central message', since 'the scope of such a system depends on the resources and energy at the centre and the capacity of the spokes' (Champion 1975). The secretariat, from the fact that the association was a federal organization, with national association members and institutional members, which were autonomous and had their own mandates from their constituencies, attempted to create itself on

a pattern whereby the various agencies working in the field [periodically] come together to thrash out issues of common import at the 'centre', which is not an institution, but this very process of consultation about a particular issue. The 'centre' is thus . . . 'a shifting' centre . . . so that the 'centre' of the model becomes, not an organisation, but a shared set of attitudes and beliefs, whose function is merely to administer, not at all to dictate, but to form the content of training and the materials for support.

(Champion 1975)

Whether and to what extent the secretariat achieved what it had intended to at its establishment should be the subject of a more exhaustive study.

THE YEARS OF TRANSFORMATION: 1982 TO 1984

This period can be described as a period of transformation. It coincided with a number of events and decisions, which had great impact on the renovation of the association's immediate objectives. Unesco had held the Minedaf Unesco Conference of ministers of education and those responsible for economic planning in Harare, Zimbabwe (1982), which had discussed the rapid expansion of all forms of education in Africa, and had resolved the eradication of illiteracy in Africa by AD 2000. Consequently Unesco's regional office in Dakar, Senegal, had carried out studies in many African countries, the analysis of whose data would help Unesco to assist governments to evolve strategies for realizing the resolutions. Emphasis was being placed on the utilization of all available resources for primary school and adult education, including literacy, for accelerating the process. African governments had found a new inspiration in using non-formal and adult continuing education programmes for turning the numerous unemployed, illiterate adults and school drop-out youth into skilled manpower for the achievement of their socio-economic national development plans. There had also occurred the years of drought, which, coming on top of the debt crisis affecting most African countries, had resulted in utter misery and famine for Africa's teeming population. The number of indigenous and foreign-aided non-governmental organizations – developmental, humanitarian, and for crisis control – had multiplied tremendously in most African countries to deal with the multifarious exigencies which were confronting Africa.

It was in the context of these events and circumstances as well as the realization that AAEA should become more involved in literacy work that the association and its sister Pan-African organization – the Afrolit Society, whose main emphasis was to promote literacy and the eradication of illiteracy in Africa – attended to the process of a merger more expeditiously than before. The Policy Statement issued by the new association – the African Association for Literacy and Adult Education – soon after the merger had been effected on 29 February 1984 addressed the major concerns confronting Africa, which its parent associations had not fully done. These major concerns were listed as the rapid population growth, underdeveloped economies and misuse of economic and natural resources, political instability, illiteracy, and ineffective social welfare and education programmes. Some of the immediate and specific objectives defined by the association, as deriving from its perception of the major concerns in Africa were

1 to increase the understanding of the people and governments of Africa on the relationship between adult literacy/adult education and the development of individuals, communities, and nations;
2 to help create voluntary national adult and literacy associations where they do not exist;

3 to strengthen the professional, organizational, and management capabilities of the voluntary adult and literacy educations in order to achieve the capacity to design and execute meaningful educational and developmental projects for the benefit of their communities;

4 to encourage the development and implementation of relevant and effective adult, continuing, literacy, vocational, and environmental education programmes in Africa.

The new association was to emphasize not only the relationship between adult education and socio-economic development in Africa but also and more than before to ensure that adult education programmes in theory and practice address the major concerns confronting Africa and contribute to their amelioration. The association would stress more than before that adult literacy and education providers not only should assume the relationship between the practice of their profession and development but also should consciously develop the contents of their programmes in order to accelerate economic development; to strengthen social programmes; to enable individual peoples to fulfil their personal ambitions as well as to contribute more positively to the well-being of their communities; to reduce disease, ignorance, and political instability; and to inculcate responsible behaviour and conduct in individuals for the various aspects of community living. The new strategies evolved by the new association, as arising out of the new perceptions of the role of adult education in Africa, included the designing and implementing of in-country and sub-regional projects which would provide member associations and other NGOs with adult and literacy education components to acquire management skills for the organization of successful adult and continuing education activities; the planning, implementing, and evaluating these programmes; the proper management of available local resources; the integration of adult education activities into other socio-economic development programmes; and the appropriate collaboration with governments and other non-governmental agencies involved in work with adults.

The new association was articulating new and immediate objectives always subsumed under the ultimate objectives, but never really concretized in programmes. These new perceptions and their implications led to the planning for continent-wide needs survey and assessment in 1986 which will assist the new association in undertaking those programmes which address the major concerns confronting African countries; meet the needs of individual national member associations; and at the same time advance the realization of the ultimate objectives, which the African Adult Education Association had enunciated at its birth.

ACTIVITIES

During the formative years, that is between 1968 and 1978, because the 'secretariat' was itinerant, being located where the honorary secretaries, who were all directors of university institutes of adult education, worked and had their own responsibility for the development and organization of their discipline within their universities, the association's activities were limited to the biennial conferences attended mainly by academicians and a few practitioners, also mainly in the top echelons of the public service; and the periodic issues of a newsletter. These conferences, which dealt with Training for Adult Education (1969), Adult Education and National Development (1971), Adult Education and the Development of Skilled Manpower (1973), and the Relationship between Formal Education and Non-Formal Education (1975), provided much substance, which both contributed to the development of adult education thought and practice in Africa and provided material for the training of adult educators. The officers of the association carried the torch of advocacy with governments and donor agencies, which in time led to the securing of funds for the establishment of the secretariat.

The establishment of the secretariat ushered in the years of growth of the association's work and expansion in the continent. In order to realize the ultimate objectives of the association and because the association had not provided for the establishment of a secretariat in its constitution, two specific practical objectives for the secretariat's responsibilities were enunciated:

1 to plan suitable programmes for trainers based on their own practical experiences and community needs;
2 to promote the creation of networks of communication, horizontally between agencies (through their participants) in various kinds of adult education activities and vertically between the trainers trained under the programmes and the grassroots in their nations.

71

The secretariat's main activity lay in the execution of regional and sub-regional workshops and three biennial conferences (each of which had a seminar incorporated as an essential component), on subjects determined by the members during the preceding biennial general meetings. The general aims of these workshops were to develop the skills of middle-level adult education practitioners and to assist trainers to initiate training at the lower levels and bring innovative ideas into their work. The participants were nominated by their national associations or affiliated institutions. The workshops were planned with the 'rippling down' or 'multiplier' effect in view: it was expected that nominating national associations and institutions would use the participants as resource persons to replicate, with appropriate modifications reflecting local conditions, similar workshops and programmes at national level so that the benefit and knowledge gained by participants will be diffused. University institutes of adult education and departments of adult education provided the bulk of resource persons for the workshops, whose venues were determined by the availability of relevant human and material resources and at the invitation of national associations and governments.

Over the period of eight years up to 1985, three sub-regional conferences and twenty-two sub-regional workshops, involving participants from thirty-six African countries, had been held. Subjects for these meetings included Evaluation, Participatory Research, Training and Research for High-Level Personnel, Environmental Education through Adult Education Programmes, Management of Associations by Secretaries and Treasurers, Responsibilities of Directors and Teachers of Part-Time Adult Education Courses, Creative Writing, Womens Education and Development: Leadership Training, Mass Media, and Adult Education, Problems and Trends in Adult Education, Radio Learning Campaigns, Strategies for the Establishment of a National Association, Integrated Community Education, Planning and Production of Post-Literacy Materials, and Management of NGOs in Africa.

Two other instruments which were planned to be used but were not appreciably realized because of a number of constraints were Research and Feasibility Studies, and Documentation. The purpose of the Research and Feasibility Study Programme was threefold: to give on-the-job training to middle-level and high-level practitioners in research methodology; to provide data for the development of training programmes in new areas at all levels to members of the association; and lastly to provide sources of knowledge on various aspects of adult education for the training of adult education students in university and other training institutions. As envisaged, a number of research subjects were determined by the association's membership for executing through participatory or action-oriented methods and procedures, but lack of financial support militated against the fulfilment of the programmes. In the area of Documentation the same constraint limited the sale of reports of workshops and conferences and the journal, which would have derived a modest income to the association. Nevertheless the free distribution of these publications and the newsletter contributed both to the diffusion of ideas and innovative experiences and methodology on the development of adult education in Africa and the promotion of the knowledge of the association education in Africa and the world.

ACHIEVEMENTS

The first concrete achievement which is immediately evident was the rapid growth of the association within and without Africa: the number of national associations had increased from 8 in 1978 to 19 in 1984; affiliated institutions from 38 in 1978 to 167 in 1984 in 32 African countries; and individual members from 200 in 1978 to 832 in 1984 in 38 African countries. Nearly 900 people from 36 countries had participated in the workshop/conference programmes of the association. The association, originally restricted to English-speaking countries, had become known in French- and Portuguese-speaking countries. All African governments knew of the association and its objectives, and were regularly invited to participate in its activities. A number of them made modest subventions to the association and many hosted its activities in their countries, affording material and human resources as well as hospitality.

On the international scene, the association had gained a professional status, participating in all international conferences in adult education and relating to the United Nations organizations, especially with Unesco, with which it had a Category B Observer Status. The association, as a vigorous and indigenous Pan-African organization, took active participation in the deliberations of the International Council for Voluntary Agencies; became involved in programmes of its humanitarian and developmental agencies; and spearheaded its management training programmes for NGOs in Africa. Through the same body, the association became a member of the World Bank/NGO Committee and with other regional NGOs entered into discussions and dialogue with the World Bank on ways in which the latter could ultimately make direct grants towards NGO programmes in the Third World.

On other aspects of the association's programmes, an Evaluation Exercise which took place in 1982 provided a number of comments up till that year:

1 On the *training of trainers* in programmes based on their own practical experience and community needs, which especially in respect of conferences was criticized as 'big jamborees and mainly an opportunity for the academics to talk to each other', the report stated that 'the academic orientation appears to have decreased in recent conferences (and workshops) but it is still important given the university origins of the AAEA and the increasing interest in adult education in African universities'.

2 On *participants at AAEA workshops and conferences*, where the criticism had been that these were 'only meant for heads of departments, who have the opportunities to communicate with each other rather than middle-level or front-line workers' and 'favouring a small group who consistently received invitations to AAEA activities', the report stated that the criticisms were 'partially valid: heads of departments are participants in AAEA events and their presence is useful in furthering AAEA aims at national and international levels. Some acknowledged that they do have other opportunities to meet each other and that it is also important that others also attend AAEA workshops and conferences'. In fact up to 1982 only 13 per cent out of 358 participants who had attended the ten AAEA conferences and workshops had been from universities, and these had been nominated by their national and institutional members.

3 On the *development of the skills of the middle-level adult educators*, the criticisms had been that the workshops had been 'planned from outside, without adequate involvement of local educators; being under-prepared; an over-reliance on lecturers; non-participatory in nature; and regional rather than national'. The report stated: 'These criticisms appear to us to be partially valid; however, AAEA Workshops have varied greatly and some are reported to have been excellent. AAEA Workshops have been planned in consultation with the Programme Committee

(set up during the 1978 Conference), and with the Administrative Committee since 1980. Details of each workshop have been worked out with host Institutions and the resource persons recommended by the hosts. The provisional programme of each workshop is discussed, modified, and finalized at the beginning of each Workshop/Conference by the participants. The criticism of outside planning is not comprehensible. . . . All Workshops have been "participatory" involving both the participants and resource persons most of whom know the methodology of adult education. Only *two* of the group of Workshops in 1978–79 had resource persons who reverted to "talk and chalk" lecturing. Subsequent Workshops have avoided as much as possible this methodology'.

4 On *usefulness of AAEA activities*, of which training workshops formed the greatest component, the Evaluation Report produced the following analysis:

Usefulness of AAEA activities	% (n=51)
nil	2.0
slightly	5.9
quite	35.3
extremely	56.8
	100.0

'In all, these training workshops have given skills related to their theories and also on facilitation, generally through sharing of experience'.

5 On the *'multiplier effect' and replication of workshops*, the Evaluation Report stated: 'These Workshops have been intended to introduce people to certain ideas with the hope that participants working through and with their national organization would organize national workshops on these topics if they think they are relevant to their situation. . . . In a number of cases there have been discussions over the possibility of organizing some local workshops but the constraint has been funding. However, in some places, for example, Zambia, Tanzania, Nigeria and Sudan, there have been training programmes organized following AAEA Regional Workshops. . . . In places, curricula of institutions have been changed to incorporate the workshop themes and

recommendations . . . ; from these findings we conclude that some of these workshops have had some multiplier effect. The participation in these Workshops has also helped in reviving National Associations'.

Finally, the Evaluation Report states, in *respect of responses to the questionnaire*, that 'the single most common achievement identified in the questionnaire returns were the AAEA workshops, conferences and publications'. These had been 'useful', and 'brought adult educators together' and 'had created an *esprit de corps*'; had 'united adult educators' and 'created a team that could think together about ways of tackling our social and economic problems'. For some respondents, correspondence from AAEA has been important. All these channels have contributed to members' learning of modern trends in adult education. Generally it had increased awareness about the importance of adult education in development. It has made adult education 'respectable' and increased 'mutual understanding among African countries'. It has 'helped get National Associations started' and its future achievements would depend on the 'effects of strengthening National Adult Education and increasing awareness about literacy', 'supported participatory research', and 'worked hard for the merger with Afrolit'.

THE ASSOCIATION AT WORK

The Association had four categories of membership: national associations, institutional members, associate members (that is non-African-based organizations), and life members (that is an honour and meritorious award for distinguished contribution). The supreme organ was the biennial general meeting, which delegated its responsibilities to the executive committee, consisting of thirteen members, elected on personal merit at the biennial general meetings by secret ballot, with the executive secretary as an *ex-officio* member and its secretary. The last executive committee was composed of persons from Burundi, Côte d'Ivoire (2), Ghana (2), Kenya (2), Lesotho, Liberia, Nigeria, Uganda, and Zambia – an evidence of the desire of the general membership that the association should be and seen to be continent-wide. A Kenyan-based administrative committee, comprising Kenya-resident adult educators was set up in 1978, a year after the establishment of the secretariat, to assist the executive secretary in discharging his responsibilities and to ensure that decisions of the general meetings and of the executive committee were executed. The executive committee statutorily had to meet once a year but this could not be adhered to because of financial constraints. It therefore normally met several times during each biennial conference in order to be able to decide on policy matters and programmes.

The biennial conferences and regional and sub-regional workshops, as the main instruments for the professional training of adult educators and the development of adult education thought and practice, became very useful in promoting the movement and enabling members to see different countries and their activities by providing different venues for each activity, wherever possible. For instance, the biennial conferences were held in Sudan (1969), Tanzania (1971), Ethiopia (1973), Zaire (1975), Kenya (1978), Swaziland (1980), and Côte d'Ivoire (1983). The regional and sub-regional workshops were held in Tanzania (1979, 1984), Nigeria (1981), Ghana (1981), Lesotho (1982), Zambia (1982), Lesotho (1982), Swaziland (1982), Côte d'Ivoire (1983), Burundi (1983), The Gambia (1984), Sierra Leone (1979, 1984), São Tomé and Principe (1984), Zimbabwe (1984), Cameroun (1984), Togo (1984), Mauritius (1979, 1980), and Kenya (1978, 1979 twice, 1981, and 1984). The choice of venues for the conferences and workshops was made for initiating the formation of a new association or strengthening an already existing one which needed re-invigoration, and further depended upon the invitation from a hosting national association and the disposition of its government to provide the necessary facilities, resources, and support. Kenya had the lion's share of these activities because it became a last resort venue, when original hosting countries had failed to host them. These activities were always given a great publicity in the host countries through the mass media and by the participation of government ministers in the opening and closing sessions. The association was thus able on the one hand to spread the knowledge of its objectives and the potential contribution it could make through their programmes in adult education to these countries and on the other hand to undertake a strong advocacy with governments on behalf of itself and the national associations. The visits of the executive secretary and, from 1982, the programme officer to prepare for these activities and to undertake other assignments for other organizations, for example Unesco, enabled them to visit many other countries, with the result that, even in countries where there were no members of the association, governments obtained information and the knowledge of the association and the latter's officers came into personal contact with government ministers, decision-makers, and high-level personnel in various countries.

CONSTRAINTS

The association undoubtedly could have achieved more than it had, but was faced with a number of constraints, among which the paramount were: the endemic lack of adequate financial provision, which impaired the spirit of voluntarism and therefore contributed to the weakness of national associations and the tenuous linkage between them and the secretariat; the geographical and linguistic spread of the association and its executive committee members with its implications for the linguistic differences and differing protocols and logistics; and doubts and questions raised about the need for and efficacy of a regional organization.

Lack of financial provision

The existence of the association, and especially its secretariat, had always been plagued by inadequate provision of funds for maintaining itself and developing and executing its programmes. It had been expected that the growth of membership would provide the financial base of the income derived from membership subscriptions to meet the secretariat's administrative and running costs. It was also hoped that governments would make modest annual subventions which together with income from membership fees and revenue from sale of publications would be sufficient to meet a substantial proportion of the remuneration of the personnel, which before the association's merger with the Afrolit Society consisted of six people; the recurrent expenditure; office supplies; postage, telegrams, and telex communications; and for documentation and publications. All these expectations were not fulfilled.

The deteriorating economic circumstances which occurred in many African countries during the late 1970s and early 1980s brought in their trail stringent exchange control in those countries, which prevented member associations, institutions, and individuals from remitting their subscriptions. The currencies of many African countries were inconvertible and it was illegal to export them. African governments would not provide the modest annual subventions of £2,000, which the association had requested from them. In the sixteen years of its existence, only two African governments made cash subventions once in respect of one country and twice in respect of the other. Governments' support was in the form of in-kind contribution in the free provision of facilities, personnel, and transportation to the association when its activities took place in their countries. The association had, therefore, to rely solely on one external donor, the Canadian International Development Agency, throughout its entire existence for funds to meet its secretarial and core administration costs, and this support had been made possible through the efforts of the International Council for Adult Education, with its headquarters based in Toronto, Canada. Other donor agencies were interested only in funding programmes and not in supporting the maintenance of the institutional structure and the remuneration of the personnel which made possible the execution of these programmes.

The association had always understood that funding for programmes would be through the sale of programmes to interested donor agencies. The achievements of the association in its programmes were, therefore, mainly due to the generosity of donor agencies, with the Canadian International Development Agency again being the biggest provider, followed by the German Adult Education Association and other international governmental/non-governmental agencies and organizations: Joseph Rowntree Trust (UK), Commonwealth Secretariat, Unesco, UNEP, British Council, Dulverton Trust (UK), Leverhulme Trust (UK), Rockefeller Foundation, USAID, ARLO, UN Voluntary Fund for Women's Decade, Norad, Danida, PACT, WHO, Ford Foundation, ICCO, ICVA, ICAE and ICEA, World Literacy of Canada, and so on. Of the grand total of Kshs. 13,749,517 raised outside Africa, Kshs. 6,941,549 came from CIDA. The cash equivalent of the in-kind contribution of African countries cannot be estimated to be more than 5 per cent of the grand total over the period. While no untoward influence was exerted on the direction and orientation of the association's programmes by donor agencies, the utter dependence of an association, which prided itself as being indigenous and authentic, made its existence very precarious since funding could be assured only annually. This short-term financing subjected the secretariat staff to unremitting and gruelling efforts in selling its programmes annually, always in doubt as to its continuing survival, since there loomed the possibility of cessation of support from donor agencies, many of which at the time of the merger were moving away from support to regional to bilateral and country organizations.

The spirit of voluntarism

The spirit of voluntarism had been one of the planks upon which national associations and the AAEA had been formed. The notion was that there was a moral obligation on the part of 'educated' people to donate freely of their time and expertise to assist in executing education and literacy programmes for the illiterate adults in their countries. This spirit had inspired the founders of the association and enabled the increase in membership of national associations to include persons from various disciplines and professions, trades, and vocations other than in the formal adult education and associated fields. With the numerical increase in the members of national associations and institutions at the national levels, it was hoped that the validity of their mission and their influence would accelerate the development and the cause of adult and literacy programmes in their countries and their adequate funding by their governments. Indeed, it had been hoped that through the membership and the activities of the association and its members, African governments would develop the political will which would produce sustained financing, planning, and execution of programmes to eradicate illiteracy and afford continuing education programmes for neo-literate adults. It was, further, hoped that the national associations, having received financial subventions from their governments, would remit a proportion annually to the secretariat for its operations. The short years of the existence of AAEA have shown that the spirit of voluntarism quickly dissipates, when it is not backed with adequate financial provision. Most enthusiastic associations and institutional members have become moribund because they had been unable to generate funds from within their membership or from their governments, or even to obtain the latter's support for soliciting funds from external agencies for their programmes.

National associations have generally grown weaker and weaker after an enthusiastic start for these reasons, except in a few notable instances, like Ghana (for a period), Zambia, and Sierra Leone, where the German Adult Education Association, through agreements with the governments of these countries, have provided grants for the execution of programmes and projects, mutually determined, designed, and developed. In Nigeria, where the government has consulted the National Council in the preparation of its periodic national development plans, activities have not been able to reach the middle level or the grassroots from lack of financial and human resources. Tanzania, because of the political decision taken by the government on adult education and the subsequent mobilization of all national resources towards the execution of its programmes, has an active and strong national association. The national associations of the countries mentioned have been able to form branches in provinces and districts of their countries, which, in turn, have strengthened them in the participatory character of their programmes and in improving their finances. In such a general situation where most national associations are languid, it had been the role of the AAEA on the one hand not only to seek funds for the continued existence of its secretariat but also to finance the involvement of participants of national associations in AAEA's programmes; and on the other hand, the AAEA had to be the advocate on behalf of national associations with their own governments. It does seem that (1) unless adult education programmes of national associations are integrated with income-generating and developmental projects; and (2) unless governments accept the programmes of adult education and approve and include them in national development plans and associations therefore are supported to seek funds with the blessing of governments, the noble and altruistic objectives of the association and its founder members cannot be fully realized.

The weak linkage between national associations and the secretariat

The general lack of funds for programmes which have rendered most national associations weak for the tasks they had planned to undertake was compounded by other factors: the scattering of their executive committees' members, which made it difficult for them to meet in order to act promptly on their associations' matters; the occurrence of a leadership vacuum in a number of associations; instances of leadership struggles stemming from different approaches to the organization of the associations' affairs; and the development of ambitious plans that attempted expensive and complicated projects with limited resources. These factors within national associations impinged upon their ability to maintain ready and continuous links with the secretariat. While no formal structure had been formed to govern the relationship between the secretariat and the member associations on the former's establishment, attempts were made, through letters, circulars, publications, and visits to develop a two-way communication channel. Attempts were made by the secretariat to involve national and institutional members in the formulation of AAEA programmes, but these did not fully succeed because of the general weakness on the part of many associations and especially from lack of core of permanent or part-time staff to handle their day-to-day correspondence, to supervise their own activities within the countries, and to correspond more regularly with the secretariat. The tenuity of the line of communication from the associations to the secretariat made it always appear that the national associations and institution members were not being involved in the development and execution of AAEA programmes. Strategies for overcoming this deficiency and establishing a free two-way flow of information and communication between the AAEA, through its secretariat, and its members were being discussed and devised on the eve of the merger, and hopefully these will be introduced and sustained by the new association.

Geographical spread of the members of the association and its implications

The geographical vastness of Africa and the resulting spread of the association, at the time of its merger with the Afrolit Society, covering 19 national associations in 17 countries, 167 institutional members in 32 African countries, and 832 individual members in 38 countries give some idea of the several problems which confronted the secretariat: linguistic differences, administrative styles, logistical and financial implications. The association had originated from the English-speaking countries and there was the urgent need to make it truly Pan-African. This meant attempting to reach the French- and Portuguese-speaking countries. The first regional workshop undertaken in late 1978 revealed three main handicaps: first, the cost was very prohibitive from the reason of the need of interpreters and translators; second, the lack of spontaneity in discussions among participants through interpreters – spontaneity being an important element for the success of practical workshops; and third, the cost of air travel for participants from different sub-regions. From this experience, the African region had to be organized into five language sub-regions for its workshops – one each for the English-speaking West, East, and Central/Southern Africa, and for French-speaking West and Central Africa. This arrangement reduced costs by eliminating the expenditure of employing interpreters/translators and enabled personal contacts and exchanges among participants from countries in each sub-region to be established; but the objective of enabling personal contacts and dialogue across linguistic barriers could not be achieved except during the biennial conferences, when both the regional workshops and the general meetings had to be conducted with simultaneous interpretation.

The spread of the members of the executive committee in Burundi, Côte d'Ivoire, Ghana, Kenya, Lesotho, Liberia, Nigeria, Uganda, and Zambia implied the provision of a considerable budget for its annual statutory meetings, the funds for which the association could not generate from within nor be obtained from external donor agencies who were not convinced of the importance of regular annual executive committee meetings for directing the affairs of the association.

Administrative procedures

The administrative styles of a number of countries required that the nomination of individuals for participation in workshops be processed through governmental procedures for official approval. Since such a procedure defeated one of the fundamental principles of an NGO, the association had to exercise tact and diplomacy to circumvent it. It was equally difficult to form voluntary national associations in the French- and Portuguese-speaking countries without the direct involvement of the appropriate government ministry and department. The association and its secretariat had to develop strategies to accommodate this procedure and still develop the voluntary spirit by requesting national commissions for Unesco in these countries to be convenors of such councils and to ensure that NGOs in the country and government departments were equally involved in the formation of an association.

Logistics

· The logistics for promoting the association in the region have proved an arduous task for both the secretariat and its members. Easy road transportation among many African countries is rare and tedious to undertake, and therefore almost all travel by participants has to be accomplished by air, which in Africa is not only expensive but also slow, time-consuming, and wearying: because of few direct and straight transits, a participant for instance from Dakar, Senegal, would have to stay one or two nights en route to Nairobi, Kenya.

Added to this is the requirement for a visa required for entry into each country, which may become an almost insuperable hurdle in the way of movement and participation of members in workshops or for visits unless prior arrangements have been made with the host country's immigration authorities. Postal communications among the countries are also expensive and slow, and most urgent communication from the secretariat, especially in connection with ensuring the receipt of air-tickets and other instructions for assembling participants for a workshop/conference, is normally carried by telegrams and telexes, which are slightly less expensive than postage. The expansion, therefore, of the association in the whole of sub-Saharan Africa has been achieved through a combination of personal visits of officers – honorary and full-time – from the secretariat and the association; through the issues of the newsletter and the journal; and through the workshops and conferences.

Is a regional organization necessary? And a secretariat?

In these days of economic hardship and the emphasis of external donors on 'grassroots' income-generating and self-reliant projects, doubts are being raised about the need of regional organizations in general. In the context of literacy and adult education, Unesco has stated clearly that the eradication of illiteracy demands a political decision by governments backed by the mobilization and utilization of all available material and human resources in each country and collaboration between governments and non-governmental organizations towards achieving the objective. Unesco has welcomed the establishment of regional organizations in adult education in all regions because they promote the spirit of voluntarism, the donation of free service of time and expertise, the mobilization of public support and opinion, the creation of solidarity of both the literate and illiterate populations for the success of the struggle against illiteracy. A regional organization like AAEA never hoped to accomplish what is best done by a national association or government department at a national level, but because the subject of illiteracy and its accompanying bane of ignorance, disease, and poverty are so pervasive and have global dimensions, its eradication cannot be accomplished in compartmentalizing the activities and programmes within each country. On this account, Unesco, on the direction of its member states, has been convening regional seminars, technical meetings, and conferences for obtaining global approaches and strategies. These inter-governmental meetings have always called for the active support of the ordinary 'educated' adults in their countries and within the region, and this desire has been the ultimate objective of national associations and the African Adult Education Association and remains that of its successor, African Association for Literacy and Adult Education.

The members of the African Adult Education Association would wish to think that it had, during its short existence, been able to sensitize public opinion and governments of Africa to the bane of illiteracy; provided advocacy for literacy and adult education before governments; mobilized qualified and interested people to give freely of their time, expertise, and service to the cause; created a forum for exchange of experiences and innovative methods for the benefit of practitioners in the service of governments in the region; and given training to trainers of trainers for work in their different countries. The successes and failures of the African Adult Education Association can be properly assessed only by an evaluation exercise. Nevertheless, a glance at the numerical growth and the geographical expansion of the association can be attributed only to the establishment of a secretariat, which could concretize the ideas of the association into programmes and raise funds for execution, through which its existence and programmes became known and were participated in by the people throughout all the countries of sub-Saharan Africa despite the different ideologies, languages and cultural barriers, and vast distances.

REFERENCES

Bown, L. and Olu Tomori, S.H. (eds) (1979) *A Handbook of Adult Education for West Africa*, London: Heinemann University Library for Africa.

Champion, A. (1975) 'Towards an ontology of adult education', *Studies in Adult Education* 7, 1, April, NIE.

Etherington, A. and Odumbe, J.A. (1982) *Final Report of the Evaluation of African Adult Education Association to AAEA Executive Committee and International NGO Division of CIDA*, Nairobi, Kenya: AAEA.

Okedera, J.I. and Stanford, R. (eds) (1974) *The Role of Adult Education in Community Development*, Ibadan, Nigeria: NNCAE.

Ulzen, E.A. (1983) 'Adult education: regional organisation in Africa', in *Encyclopedia of Education: Research and Studies*, London: Pergamon.

—— (1985) 'Experiences of other professional bodies in the professionalisation of their vocation – the case of the African Adult Education Association', *Journal of the African Adult Education Association* 1, Nairobi, Kenya.

Ulzen, E.A. and Wangoola, P. (1983) 'Purpose, target and trends in African Adult Education Association's training programme', *Journal of the African Adult Education Association* 1, 3, Nairobi, Kenya.

Wandira, A. (1971) *Indigenous Education in Uganda*, Kampala: Makerere University.

Other sources: Historical note on AAEA and its 1978–83 Programme of Activities.

The Constitution of African Adult Education Association.

The Policy Statement of the African Association for Literacy and Adult Education.

Unesco publications.

7

The European Bureau of Adult Education

Derek Legge

ORIGINS AND EARLY DAYS

The origins of the European Bureau of Adult Education lie in the ferment of opinion just after the Second World War. Many Europeans felt an almost desperate need to build up contacts and to open channels of communication through which, it was hoped, a more closely knit Europe would develop. Some in fact wanted to create a totally unified Europe, though the complexity and difficulties of such a dream were soon revealed by the many disagreements about the kinds of structures which might be necessary. Even so in the years just after 1945, both individuals and groups tried to press forward, and a varied multitude of agencies came into being. Some of these attempts to develop international contacts were short lived and torn apart by ideological differences while others enjoyed a longer and more fruitful existence. Among these were the International Federation of Settlements and Neighbourhood Centres and the European Youth Campaign, which set up its secretariat in Paris in 1952. An important move forward had also come when the European Federalist Movement, despite persistent displays of disunity, organized a Congress in May 1948 in The Hague. This produced two resolutions, one of which led to the establishment of the Council of Europe in 1949 and the other to the inauguration of a European Cultural Centre in Geneva in October 1950.

As might be expected, goodwill was mixed with much muddled thinking and ideological friction, and some countries, such as the United Kingdom, tended to be suspicious of all attempts to secure European co-operation. Moreover the education of adults tended to have a priority lower than most other matters, and the number of full-time 'adult educators', however defined, in Europe was but small – according to some, just a band of perhaps two dozen activists. There were also suspicions and antagonisms between workers in the various sectors of the work, residential provision being set against non-residential, community work against formal classes, and so on, and it was believed by some that the right way forward was contact confined to one sector only. Thus in 1952 meetings of the European Cultural Centre led to efforts to create a European Secretariat of Community Centres. Nevertheless these meetings also brought suggestions for an independent body which would include representatives of all adult education organizations and which might be called a European Council for Adult Education. The name was not found to be acceptable to all, but a provisional executive committee was nominated, and this met for the first time on 30 November 1953.

This committee proceeded to take some vital decisions and, although no legal basis was then created, the meeting is rightly regarded as the foundation of the European Bureau of Adult Education. The first decisions indeed settled the name, arguments raging as to whether it should be 'European' or 'international', a 'bureau' or a 'council'. The committee also agreed a provisional structure in the form of a steering committee and an annual general membership conference. It also discussed finance, if with more hope than precision. A new international organization of adult educators was being formed, despite divergent viewpoints about the amount of independence it should have as well as sectoral divisions, and the existence of some potential rivals such as the European Circle of Friends of Peoples' Colleges and the Communauté des Anciens de Mondsee-Marly, the latter being a group of adult educators which had first met at the Unesco Mondsee Seminar (1950). The future in fact was far from clear and some adult educators were very guarded in their response. One of these, indeed, was Edward Hutchinson, the secretary of the National Institute of Adult Education (England and Wales) who later became an enthusiastic supporter and the active and devoted first president of the bureau. (For a full account of the origins see Schouten 1978: 3–20.)

If the new organization was to survive amid the conflicts, it had to develop both the support of the main educators of adults in Europe, and a satisfactory structure. Early support came from individuals such as Albert Léger of France, Frank Milligan of Britain, and Oscar Guermonprez of the Netherlands, but the decisive role was undoubtedly played by G.H.L. (Bob) Schouten. Born in 1906, he undertook youth work in the Netherlands from the mid-1920s onwards and in 1951 became both principal of the Rockanje Folkhighschool and secretary of the European work of the Association of Dutch Folkhighschools. With Oscar Guermonprez, he had attended the meetings of the European Cultural Centre and of the European Youth Campaign, and when the new 'provisional executive committee' was formed he was asked to become its honorary secretary. Committed to the European ideal, he strove with great persistence to build co-operation whatever the difficulties. At ease in English, French, and German as well as his native Dutch, he brought adult educators together in a kind of international comradeship, and his devoted attention to detail as well as his cheerful optimism enabled the bureau to continue to grow even in a world which tended to become more divided. The Association of Dutch Folkhighschools gave great help by allowing him the freedom to run the affairs of the bureau alongside its own work but he never failed to carry out both tasks with great efficiency. Even after his nominal retirement from his Dutch post in 1971, he continued to work hard for the cause he loved and it is not surprising that his favourite quotation was taken from A. de Saint Exupery: 'Le plus beau métier des hommes est d'unir les hommes' (see Hutchinson 1981: 51–2). The immense respect which he rightly earned led, after his death in 1981, to the foundation of the 'Bob Schouten Fund', which exists to help young educators of adults to travel and study adult education in one of the countries of Europe.

The development of real personal friendships resulting from the contacts created by the bureau has been of great importance in helping it to overcome many of the problems it has faced. Among these has been the ever-present question of the definition of 'adult education' which has had peculiarly European features not greatly helped by the use of the term *éducation permanente* by the Council of Europe. The 'European idea' tended to evoke either suspicions or apathy, and progress was often blocked by 'barriers of language, custom and unhappy memories of things past' (Hutchinson 1973: 40). Organizations were often reluctant to forge good links and the divisions of east and west were emphasized by the phases of the Cold War. Inside the bureau there were recurrent problems concerning the constitution, the aims, and the objectives as well as the continuing search for financial support. Under Bob Schouten's influence, however, the bureau steadily developed its work of giving help and advice and of bringing people together in study tours and conferences. It has been said that the bureau did this often enough to give a human and personal dimension to the idea of co-operation in a way which was not possible for inter-governmental bodies such as the United Nations, surrounded as they have been by the exigencies of protocol (Hutchinson 1973: 40).

MEMBERSHIP AND OBJECTIVES

Like many voluntary, non-governmental organizations, the bureau has been dependent on the work and commitment of a relatively small group of individuals. Full-time educators of adults in Europe tended to form a tight network of friends who found experience in the work of the bureau greatly stimulating. Gradually, however, as they built up the organization they came to feel that it was of vital importance to develop the widest possible membership. From their discussions has emerged a constitution which provides for the affiliation of organizations active at all levels, 'local, regional, national and international'. Primarily these 'associates' are the national organizations for which the bureau is a kind of umbrella, but there are also regional or local bodies in membership including individual institutions. In the early days of the bureau national agencies or institutes in many countries were often either weak or non-existent and one of the tasks of the bureau has been to help their formation and to strengthen them. Today they form the backbone of the bureau which has come to be very dependent on their support, despite the growing number of sub-national bodies which have been admitted. In 1985, for example, there were 160 associates drawn from 19 countries. Although essentially an organization of organizations, the bureau has also specially admitted a tiny number of individual associates, people who are regarded as having made a special contribution to European adult education – 'individuals having particular knowledge and experience . . . but not otherwise eligible' for membership (Constitution 4.1.8.).

The aims of the bureau are defined in the Constitution (section 2.1.) as being

to facilitate development in the field of adult education, to encourage discussions of adult educators to gain a better understanding of the great problems of their time, and to encourage co-operation between adult education agencies in the different countries of Europe.

In seeking to achieve these it has tried hard to retain the flexibility which Bob Schouten declared to be 'one of the pre-conditions for the full functioning of a European Bureau' (Schouten 1970: 74). Until relatively recently, however, most of its associates have come from the northern and central parts of western Europe and, despite friendly contact with representatives of countries in eastern Europe, institutional membership from there has never developed. Links with southern Europe, however, are now more promising, especially as national agencies have come into being in the Mediterranean region. Italy, Spain, Portugal, and Cyprus have recently come into membership and the bureau continues to do much both to facilitate contacts between their agencies and to stimulate general co-operation between north and south. A further development has been the admission of Israel in 1983 after consideration of the definition of the 'European region' by Unesco and by the International Council for Adult Education. In general it has cast a wide net and, as Titmus has said, 'it is possible for a wider range of adult educators to participate actively in its work than in that of UNESCO, the OECD or the Council of Europe' (Titmus 1981: 221). The encouragement of mutual awareness has been one of its major achievements.

ORGANIZATION

The affairs of the bureau are managed by the steering committee which tries to be as representative as possible. Nowadays it has delegates from each of the national co-ordinating bodies of similar agencies, together with five members elected by the general assembly and up to five co-opted members. Co-option is used to improve the representation of functional or geographical interests. The steering committee has thus become a sizeable body, and in 1985, for example, it had twenty-one members. It meets about twice a year, often in the Netherlands, and it is responsible for the appointment of the officers by the bureau – the president, vice-presidents, secretary-treasurer, and 'such other officers as may be deemed necessary' (Constitution 7.1). Although power thus rests with the steering committee, the general assembly, which first met in 1958, gives it advice, and discusses both the broad lines of policy and the general progress of the work. It meets usually every two years, although the Constitution now states 'at no more than three year intervals', and it is composed of all associates, all with the power to vote except for the few individual associates. At an earlier date much use was made of sub-committees often limited to one sector though appointed by the steering committee, but these are now a rarity.

In 1964 the bureau at last became a legal entity and was registered as a foundation according to Dutch law. Bob Schouten continued his unpaid work as its honorary secretary nearly up to his death in 1981 but he constantly pressed for the establishment of a permanent paid post as the major staffing need of the future. Thanks to the generous support of the Dutch government this became possible in 1977 when the steering committee appointed Willem (Bill) Bax as the bureau's first full-time director. Mr Bax had been deputy secretary for some years following his work in the special Meeting Europe project from 1968 onwards. The Dutch government had in fact given a substantial annual subsidy to the bureau from 1963 onwards and in 1977 was covering about half the bureau's budget. Originally this subsidy had been intended as a 'primer' to help the bureau to become established and it was to last until other European countries took up their share with appropriate contributions, an optimistic objective which has been difficult to secure. The financial problem became acute when in 1982, under economic stress, the Dutch subvention began to be withdrawn and the bureau again found itself unable to maintain a full-time director. Arrangements were made in 1983, however, for Mr Bax to continue to serve the bureau but on a part-time basis while being employed for 60 per cent of his time by the Dutch National Centre of Adult Education (NCVO). The Dutch National Centre has been of considerable help to the bureau over the years and in 1971 the bureau's office was transferred to the same building in Amersfoort, where it could use the centre's extensive documentation and library services.

After the establishment of the International Council for Adult Education in 1973, the bureau took up membership as a regional organization while retaining its independence. Since 1970 it has also become directly associated with the Salzburg Discussions of Leaders in Adult Education, which are organized each year by the Verband Österreichischer Volkshochschulen. In general, despite all the tensions and crises of the years since 1953, the bureau has set an example in stimulating co-operation wherever it seemed possible, and the flexible constitution has been of much help in disarming the opposition and strong reservations of various groups of adult educators. As Edward Hutchinson said at a very early date (Hutchinson 1957: 120)

> The value of the bureau lies precisely in the ability of its sponsors to see adult education as a means of examining and interpreting issues of great importance, including that of European unity, without taking sides in the controversies that necessarily surround them.

ACTIVITIES

Conferences

Although the stress on co-operation has always been present, the activities of the bureau, like its constitution, have developed in ways not always foreseen. However, throughout its life, conferences and other meetings have been obvious ways of trying to achieve the objectives eventually laid down in the constitution as being 'to develop the competence of adult educators' (2.2.4.) and 'to stimulate public action and pressure for the further development of adult education' (2.2.3.).

In the early days, the themes were mainly work in residential adult education, or in rural development, or the problems of European co-operation. Seven conferences on rural reconstruction were held between 1953 and 1969 in the Netherlands, Germany, Italy, and England, and no fewer than fourteen were held on residential adult education between 1951 and 1973, an almost annual event in the 1950s. The Adult Education Association of the USA joined in the organization of three of these (1957, 1959, 1962) and in all there was support from the local adult education organizations and the government of the country in which the conference was held. Between 1954 and 1958 there were also five conferences in Bergen (N.H.) on Adult Education in Europe, organized in co-operation with the Dutch Foundation for the European Work of the Folk High Schools (Stichting voor Europees Volkshogeschoolwerk) and supported by the Dutch government. Up to 1954 these activities were strictly the concern of the European Secretariat of the Dutch Folk High Schools but they were then willingly transferred to be the direct responsibility of the bureau. Bob Schouten was, of course, the secretary of both organizations.

There were early signs of a need to diversify the themes and to extend the range of sponsorship. When in the 1960s the Council of Europe began to take a wider interest in adult education, several meetings were organized by the bureau in co-operation with the council, and the aid of the European Communities as well as that of national governments was actively pursued. An early example of a multi-sponsored conference was that in 1961 when, with the support of the European Communities, the Dutch government, and the Prinz Bernhard Foundation, meetings were held in Brussels and Bergen (N.H.) the theme of the conference being the training of professional workers in adult education. In the following year, near Munich, a conference on training and on relationships with the media had the support of the West German government and the active co-operation of the German Adult Education Association (Deutscher Volkshochschul-Verband). A sector on 'non-residential' adult education also began to develop, the first conference on this theme taking place in Haus Rief, near Salzburg, in 1964, where the main concern was recruitment to the evening institutes. A second conference in Hanover in 1965 looked at the types of subjects offered in evening institutes and a third in Moor Park College, England (1966) discussed a wide range of contemporary developments.

Other themes also appeared. A conference at Marly-le-Roi in France in 1955 looked at the Cultural and Social Needs of a Large City while others included the Ideological Discussion with the East (1960) and Adult Education in a Changing Context of Work and Leisure (1967). On the whole these conferences tended to discuss practical experiences and problems and to bring information about practical developments in various countries to the attention of the associates. Some were linked to the general assemblies, and even though the general theme of the first of these at Marly-le-Roi in 1958 was declared to be 'the essential elements of a European culture and a European spirit in adult education', more attention was given to the ciné-clubs of France and to practical work in the UK and Germany. These conferences gave adult educators good opportunities in which to deepen their understanding of achievements and ideas outside their own countries, and they also brought contact with representatives of countries not easily reached because of ideological issues. An interesting development was a series of international summer courses on the theme Meeting Europe held from 1962 to 1971 with the support of the European Cultural Foundation. These were designed to bring young adults from different countries together in a residential setting and in all about twenty countries took part. Although it is perhaps doubtful if they did much to promote an awareness of the cultural entity of Europe, they undoubtedly helped those taking part to gain a wider understanding as well as many international friendships. All these meetings and conferences also helped a good deal to publicize the bureau and to make it more 'visible' to governments and international agencies.

From the 1970s onwards the themes of the bureau conferences have ranged over almost all aspects of the education of adults, although they have been focused particularly on new developments. The problems of the local or regional provision of adult education have been a recurrent topic, echoing the pressures in many countries of Europe to decentralize the implementation of adult education policy. Thus they were the subject at Munster in 1977, at the twenty-fifth anniversary conference in Borne, in the Netherlands in 1978, and in Pistoia, Italy, in 1984. Information, guidance, and counselling services in adult education have frequently come under consideration and were the theme of a special conference in Berlin in 1981. Similarly there has been much concern with the implementation of legislation concerning the education of adults. Conferences specifically dealing with this and with general policy matters were held at Oslo in 1972, Marly-le-Roi in 1975, Berlin in 1979, and Södertälje in Sweden in 1984. The problems of unemployment were first examined by the bureau in 1972 and subsequently there were special meetings in Chatenay-Malabry, France, in 1979, and in Amersfoort, the Netherlands, in 1984. Attention to other special target groups has been given in conferences on the disadvantaged in Farnham, England, in 1976 and in Israel in 1981, and on adult basic education in St Andrews, Scotland, in 1983.

Meetings which have followed the first European seminar on women's education held in Wansfell College, England, in 1980, have now led to the establishment of a special network for women's education. The role of broadcasting and other media has not been ignored; a conference in Brussels in 1976 discussed the setting up of multi-media systems, one in Humlebaek, Denmark, in 1982 looked at the use of the media in local adult education, and another in Woburn, England, in 1985 considered new information technology and adult education. Older topics have not been forgotten. There was, for example, a conference on Co-operation between Residential and Non-Residential Forms of Adult Education held in Haus Buchenreid, Germany, in 1980, and one on the Training and Further Training of Adult Educators held in Geiranger, Norway, in 1982. Haus Buchenreid was also the venue for a 1985 conference on Adult Education, Health and the Quality of Life to which health educators were particularly invited. A somewhat different form of conference has been that of the occasional meetings of directors of the national institutes of adult education or similar organizations which have been held from time to time, as in 1978 and 1980, and that of the editors of adult education journals as in 1967 and 1983. The bureau has in fact been willing to promote any meeting which seems likely to assist the development of adult education, the only condition being the need for adequate financial support.

Publications

Some of the declared objectives of the bureau are 'to act as an information centre' (Constitution 2.1.), 'to make available publications in the field of adult education' (2.2.) and 'to make available documentation related to all its aims and objectives' (2.6.). In part fulfilment of these, a regular feature of the bureau's activities has been the publication of conference reports, usually put together by a guest editor, and these now form a quite impressive library. Sometimes, too, it has undertaken special reports as when in 1964 the Council of Europe commissioned the bureau to make the first comparative study of emerging policies concerning the 'status, recruitment and professional training of adult educators' in six countries, a pilot study discussed at the Strasbourg conference of the bureau in 1965. From an early date it was felt necessary to produce a periodical or newsletter, and in 1954 the first, rather modest, issue appeared of *Notes and Studies*. With the assistance of the European Youth Campaign it was published in three separate language editions but such linguistic enterprise later became financially more difficult. In 1978 it was joined by a *Newsletter* produced with the aid of the International Council for Adult Education. Funded by the ICAE, this was a project to make information about European materials and developments in adult education more accessible to North

American adult educational organizations, and vice versa. There were problems of getting a response in North America, however, and eventually financial difficulties after a decline in the value of the Canadian dollar. After the initial two years of the ICAE subsidy, therefore, the bureau took sole responsibility for the *Newsletter* and amalgamated *Notes and Studies* with it in 1981. With the help of financial support from associates, some of whom carry out the editorial work for specific issues, it has been possible to produce usually two issues a year. Often these are concerned with the themes of the conferences and attempts are made to bring them out at a time when they can provide basic documentation. In any case the *Newsletters* have become invaluable to European adult educators as a source of information about immediate practice in a wide range of educational work with adults.

The bureau has also attempted to facilitate contact by publishing some basic materials. One example is a *Directory* of European adult educational organizations. This description of the structure of adult education in various European countries is subject to regular up-dating, and although mainly concerned with western Europe, it has gradually extended its range. Similarly there are on-going attempts to improve a list of adult education terms in different languages. This began as French–German–English but now extends to Dutch and Italian. Communication between European adult educators has been beset by the problem of finding accurate equivalent meanings to words in the various languages and this list has made a significant contribution. The bureau has also completed a survey on adult education legislation in western Europe, Yugoslavia, and Israel, which was published in 1984 with the support of Unesco. As indicated above, the subject had been discussed in several conferences and publications from 1965 onwards and Unesco gave a special commission to the bureau as part of the preparation for the 1985 World Conference. The bureau has also undertaken smaller tasks such as an annual list of International Summer Courses and Conferences on Adult Education, first produced in 1959, and, with the Scottish Institute and the Netherlands Association, a *Bulletin on Feministic Educational Work for Women.* An early attempt to provide an abstracting service proved too work-intensive, and had therefore to be abandoned after a fairly short time.

PROBLEMS AND THE FUTURE

Finance has been a steady problem for the bureau throughout its life, and the absence of a secure financial basis has been a great hindrance to the development of its work. Each associate pays a membership fee adjusted according to its size, status, and position, but with the bureau's stress on the need for a wide membership, all fees have been kept as low as possible. As a result conferences have been dependent upon special subventions from other agencies or upon invitations from a host country which has then provided the necessary funds. Similarly publications have also depended on special funding or on the goodwill of associates linked to the efforts of some devoted enthusiasts. The main problem, however, lies in the core-funding, the cost of the central secretariat and equipment with which to keep the bureau in being. For most of its life the bureau relied to a large extent on the disproportionate financial support provided by the Dutch government without conditions, but after the withdrawal of much of this subsidy in recent years, the bureau has had to depend on only part-time help from its director and clerical staff. Even so it has continued a full programme of activities, although these are increasingly dependent on voluntary effort and the overloading of its willing part-time director and unpaid officers. In a real sense, of course, the bureau has only survived by the inspiration and hard work of a small number of individuals. Attempts to secure grants from various charitable foundations have brought some results but always they have been related to specific activities rather than central needs, and increased grants from European governments in the present economic climate seem a vain hope. It is clear, however, that the permanence of the bureau as an institution depends in the long run on a solution being found to the problem of central funding.

A second matter of importance for future development is the need to widen contacts in Europe. As indicated already, the bureau has done much to stimulate developments in the countries of southern Europe and to build stronger links between them and adult educators in northern Europe, and it is clear that more attention should now be given to matters such as the roles to be played by various adult educational organizations, and ways of constructing and implementing suitable programmes. Study visits have been suggested together with measures such as the further extension of the *Directory* and the greater use of French translations of bureau material. The problems of diversity, of course, continue to exist but the experience of those taking part in the activities of the bureau suggests that face-to-face encounters and the search for understanding often bring a realization of much common ground.

Ideals and ideas have changed a good deal since the early years of the bureau and Europe remains divided, reduced in world status, and far away from the old aspirations of unity and co-operation. Little seems to remain of the old enthusiasms and vision. These circumstances, however, suggest that far from destroying the basis for the bureau, there is an even greater need for it to continue. Its role in promoting contact and co-operation between educators of adults, and in providing opportunities for the exchange of ideas and the creation of real fellowship, is now more than ever vital. In the technologically advanced world of today with its ever-increasing speed of change, adult educators, in adjusting their work, can be greatly helped by an awareness of the changes in purposes, organization, and methods which are in progress in other countries. The bureau is an excellent agency for the dissemination of such information and it can provide both a forum for the discussion of opinions, however unpalatable, and a means for the encouragement of the search for common principles. Evidence of its ability to be forward looking can be seen in its new plans for a four-year project on the Education and Training of Adults in a Changing Employment Market. In general the bureau has had an excellent record of achievement, has developed much goodwill, and has a clear place as a regional force in the world of adult education. It is essential that its programme of conferences and publications continue, and with more financial support it could play an even more vital role both in Europe and in the world at large.

REFERENCES

Publications about the bureau have been relatively few (as is shown by the following list).

Bax, W. (1984) 'Adult education in regional organizations in Western Europe', in *International Encyclopedia of Education*, vol. 1, 167–9, Oxford: Pergamon.
Hutchinson, E.M. (1957) 'The European Bureau of Adult Education', *Adult Education* 30, 2: 118–21.
—— (1970) 'Thoughts after Montreal', *Convergence* 3, 2: 48–54, especially p. 52.
—— (1973) 'A case study in co-operation – the European Bureau of Adult Education', *Convergence* 4, 3 and 4: 40–2.

—— (1981)'Obituary – G.H.L. 'Bob' Schouten', *Adult Education* 54, 1: 51–2.

Schouten, G.H.L. (1970) 'European adult education ten years after the Montreal conference', *Convergence* 3, 2: 72–4, especially p. 74.

—— (1978) *The European Bureau of Adult Education, 1953–1978*, Amersfoort: EBAE (the only substantial account of the early years).

Titmus, C. (1981) *Strategies for Adult Education – Practices in Western Europe*, Milton Keynes: Open University Press, see p. 240.

See also brochures issued by the bureau, especially the thirteen-page edition of 1984, and notes on the work of the bureau provided by E.M. Hutchinson in issues of the journal *Adult Education* from 1964 to 1979.

8

The Asian-South Pacific Bureau of Adult Education

Lim Hoy Pick

THE FOUNDATION

The Unesco World Conference on Adult Education held in Montreal in 1960 brought together leading adult educators from various parts of the world. During this conference delegates from south-east Asian countries and those from Australia and New Zealand met to plan regional seminars and conferences aimed at bringing about consultation and co-operation among adult educators in the Asian-South Pacific region and at carrying on the good work of the Montreal Conference. To achieve these aims, they made two important decisions: first, to hold a conference in Saigon (then capital of South Vietnam) in 1962 on the theme Adult Education in the Urban Setting in Asia and Adult Education in the Rural Setting in Asia and, second, to hold another regional seminar two years later in Sydney, Australia, on two aspects of adult education, the Role of the School and the Role of the University in Adult Education. Both the Saigon Conference and the Sydney Seminar were successfully held as planned.

The Unesco regional seminar on the Role of Universities and Schools in Adult Education was held at the University of Sydney, Australia, towards the end of January 1964. Delegates at the seminar generally agreed that some machinery should be created to foster and facilitate continuing consultation and co-operation among adult educators in the Asian-South Pacific region. Therefore a founding meeting of the Asian-South Pacific Bureau of Adult Education (ASPBAE) was convened at the Women's College, University of Sydney, on 30 January 1964. At the closing of the meeting the following executive committee was elected:

Chairman: Shri S.C. Dutta, Secretary-General, Indian Adult Education Association

Hon. secretary: A.S.M. Hely, Director of Adult Education, University of Adelaide, Australia

Executive members: Ang Gee Bah, Director, Adult Education Board, Singapore, Malaysia

R. Gibson, Director of Education, Saipan, Mariana Islands

I.W. Hughes, Director, Department of Extra-Mural Studies, University of Hong Kong

U Kyaw Khin, Assistant Registrar, Rangoon University, Rangoon, Burma

Seiichi Okamura, Professor of Agricultural Sociology, Tokyo Agricultural Technological University, Tokyo, Japan

Tartib Prawirodihardjo, Director, Department of Community Education, Jakarta, Indonesia

A. Vizconde, Assistant Chief, Division of Adult and Community Education, Department of Education, Manila, Philippines

(ASPBAE *Minutes*, 31 January 1964: 8)

Among the well-known adult educators who attended the meeting were John Lowe (Director of Extra-Mural Studies, University of Singapore), A.J.A. Nelson (Director of Extension Services, University of New England, Australia), A.N. Charters (Dean of University College, University of Syracuse, USA), H. Dolff (Secretary-General, German Folk High School Association, Germany), S.G. Raybould (Director, Department of Extra-Mural Studies, University of Leeds, England), and P. Lengrand (Division of Adult Education and Youth Activities, Unesco). It was agreed that the new committee should establish a clearing-house, should publish, if possible, a reasonably regular newsletter, should keep in touch with post-seminar developments in the countries of the region and maintain a liaison with Unesco and international NGOs such as the World Confederation of Organizations of the Teaching Profession (WCOTP) and International Congress of University Adult Education (ICUAE), and should co-operate in arrangements for further regional conferences and seminars.

Altogether thirty-six representatives, participants, and observers attending the Sydney Seminar joined the bureau as foundation members, representing thirteen countries and territories in Asia and the South Pacific. Helmuth Dolff, general secretary of the Deutscher Volkshochschul-Verband E.V. (DVV) took out an institutional membership for his organization.

ASPBAE started without many financial resources, therefore one of the early efforts of the executive was to raise funds to finance the activities of the bureau. Despite the lack of financial resources, the membership fee was deliberately fixed at a nominal level (5 Australian shillings) in order (1) that membership would not be restricted by high fees, and (2) that payment of fees should not be hindered by rigid exchange controls in some countries in the region.

During the months immediately after the formation of the bureau, the executive was busy planning the production of a quarterly newsletter and a twice-yearly journal. Ieuan Hughes was appointed editor of the bureau's newsletter and journal. Meanwhile the chairman, Shri Siva Dutta, obtained from the Asia Foundation a grant of HK$2,870 to finance the newsletter and journal for a period of one year. The first newsletter was produced in October 1964.

Within the same year between 26 and 31 October, a conference on South-East Asian Universities and Extra-Mural Work was held at the University of Hong Kong. It was called the Leverhulme Conference because of the financial support from the Leverhulme Trust of Great Britain. ASPBAE was closely associated with the planning and conduct of the conference and partly through the participation of the ASPBAE executive members in the conference itself. The conference was attended by forty-four delegates, observers, and consultants, including representatives of fifteen South-East Asian universities, members of the ASPBAE executive, two representatives of the Association of South-East Asian Institutes of Higher Learning (ASAIHL), and two consultant specialists (W.E. Styler, Director of Adult Education, University of Hull, and G.J.A. McIntyre, Director of Extension, University of Western Ontario). In fact, the Leverhulme Conference was regarded as a follow-up of the Sydney Seminar on the Role of Universities and Schools in Adult Education. The report of the Sydney Seminar was adopted as the main working paper for discussion sessions. It should be noted that during 1964 and 1965 ASPBAE paid particular attention to the question of the participation of Asian universities in adult education. With the development in the provision of adult education services at the literacy and post-literacy level came the need for the types of services which could be made by universities, such as the training of adult literacy supervisors, teachers, and researchers. Yet universities in most Asian countries had not played a significant role in the education of adults. This weakness had been recognized and was one of the main issues discussed at such important Asian regional conferences as the Saigon Conference and Sydney Seminar. It was the main theme of the Leverhulme Conference and the most important outcome of the conference was the unanimous agreement that an Institute of Adult Education for research, teaching, and documentation services should be established in South-East Asia. It was further agreed that it should be attached to the University of Hong Kong.

Right from the beginning of ASPBAE, Arnold Hely had been particularly supportive of the adult education movement in South-East Asia. In his report on the Leverhulme Conference, he wrote:

> Moreover, Australia has a special interest in social and economic development in S.E. Asia. It has interests and recognised responsibilities in assisting S.E. Asia in its educational development. Australia has already made a valuable contribution to elementary education, teachers' training and to vocational education. There is a need for a similar contribution in the field of adult education. It is in the area of the universities' contribution to adult education that Australia can perhaps make the greatest contribution to adult education in this geographical region, for it has had a long and varied experience in university extension.
>
> (Hely 1964: 5)

By making these observations, Arnold Hely seemed to foresee what was to happen a decade later when Chris Duke of the Australian National University became the secretary-general of ASPBAE and translated his (Hely's) vision into reality.

In subsequent years until 1967, the ASPBAE executive had been very active in the promotion of adult education in the Asian-South Pacific region. After the Sydney Seminar the executive met annually in Hong Kong in 1964, Manila in 1965, New Delhi in 1966, and Singapore in 1967. As early as 1965 ASPBAE policies and views began to influence deliberations at a number of important educational conferences concerning Asia and the South Pacific through the active participation of ASPBAE members either as delegates or observers. These conferences included the World Conference on University Adult Education held at Krogerup in Denmark in June, the World Congress of Ministers of Education on the Eradication of Illiteracy held at Teheran in September, the International Conference of Universities in Japan in September, and the Conferences of Asian Ministers of Education and Planning held at Bangkok in November. Moreover, ASPBAE had established good working relationships with international organizations such as Unesco, ICUAE, and WCOTP, and several national associations and councils of adult education such as the Australian Association of Adult Education, Indian Adult Education Association, National Council of Adult Education of New Zealand, and the Bureau of Public Schools in the Philippines.

In the 1960s the Federal German Government had been sponsoring training programmes for adult education leaders from developing countries in Africa and Latin America. At the ASPBAE executive meeting held in Delhi in October 1966, Arnold Hely reported that he had discussed with Helmuth Dolff, Head of the German Association for Adult Education (DVV), the possibility of extending this German Training Programme to adult educators from developing countries in Asia. It was resolved at the Delhi meeting that the follow-up should be

1 to get a full detailed curriculum of the training programme from the German Association for Adult Education;
2 to circulate this programme to Asian ministers of education with a covering letter;
3 to send copies of correspondence to members of ASPBAE in the various Asian countries who might be in a position to support the proposals by direct approaches to their government;
4 that, in addition, ASPBAE members be asked to discuss with German embassies or legations in their own country the question of the extension of the German Training Scheme to Asia.

(ASPBAE *Minutes* 24–26 October 1966: 83–4)

After the Delhi Conference Arnold Hely visited Germany and held discussions with Helmuth Dolff and other German authorities. He found the German government sympathetic to the proposals made by ASPBAE, although its representatives felt that existing financial difficulties might delay slightly the extension of the programme to Asia. Eventually this slight delay turned out to be a long one.

Several events that took place in 1967 greatly influenced the development of adult education in the Asian-South Pacific region. In 1967 Sandy Liveright, secretary of ICUAE, visited a number of Asian countries and talked with ASPBAE members throughout Asia. He was deeply impressed by the work of ASPBAE and its potential as a regional co-ordinating organization for the Asian-South Pacific area. After the visit, he made the following recommendations:

1 the strengthening of ASPBAE through outside financial assistance;
2 development of a high-level research and training centre in adult education in South-East Asia;
3 development of a consortium of experienced and concerned adult educators in the USA, Canada, and the UK to work closely with ASPBAE and the institute proposed in (2);
4 provision of a long-term continued consultative and advisory service to key adult educators and individual countries by the above consortium;
5 foundation funding for a three- to five-year period to get the proposed programme under way.

(ASPBAE *Minutes*, 26 November 1967: 7–8)

These recommendations attracted a great deal of interest and discussion among adult educators in ASPBAE countries. But the ASPBAE executive committee faced many difficulties in their implementation, especially the one on foundation financing. For example, when Arnold Hely applied to the Asia Foundation for a grant of US$3,000 to finance secretarial assistance for three years, he secured only US$1,500 in the first instance. Ieuan Hughes faced even greater problems in getting financial assistance from the Department of Overseas Development in Britain and other foundations for the actual establishment of the proposed Institute of Adult Education to be set up at the University of Hong Kong. In his letter to Sandy Liveright on 27 October 1967, he wrote:

Hong Kong University has put an awful lot of time, effort and money into the idea [Institute of Adult Education] so far and I am sure nobody would like this to be wasted. It will require a major investment of effort, staff, preparation, running and financing. More than I think anyone has fully faced up to. Had I remained here I was determined to find some way of getting it going, though I was fully aware of the size of the burden involved, for it must be done well, and real, intelligent and practical offers of assistance have been depressingly few.

(ASPBAE Outward Correspondence)

Ieuan Hughes left Hong Kong at the end of October 1967 to take up the appointment as Warden of Coleg Harlech in North Wales. With his departure, the chapter on the proposed Institute of Adult Education came to a close.

ASPBAE had maintained close contact with Unesco particularly with the Adult Education Officer attached to the Unesco Regional Office for Education in Bangkok. Unesco had shown its interest in and sympathy for the work which the bureau was attempting to undertake in the region and was aware of the contribution such a body could make to the general purposes and objectives of Unesco in the field of adult education. It nominated T. Krishnamurthy, Unesco Technical Adviser to the Unesco Regional Office at Bangkok, to attend the ASPBAE Conference in Manila and to participate in the executive meeting held at the conclusion of the Manila Conference. Later on in June 1967, M. de Clerck was appointed Adult Education Specialist at the Unesco Regional Office for Education in Asia. Prior to this appointment, he had been posted as Unesco Chief of Mission and Adult Education Specialist in two Asian countries: Vietnam and Iran. On 21 June 1967 he wrote to Arnold Hely saying:

First of all, the Regional Office will need your valuable assistance in the building up of a documentation and information centre on adult education. It will be concerned with adult education in the broadest sense, including under this label: workers' education, social education, farmers' education, women's education, extra-mural studies as well as adult literacy. Thanks to the publications of all kinds that will be gratefully received, we hope to set up a well-documented centre that will ensure the exchange of information in the field of adult education and be available to all specialists concerned.

One other important item for which the Unesco Regional Centre wishes to enlist your support concerns the preparation of a list of leading personalities of your country dealing with the manifold aspects of adult education in the region, including literacy, reading materials, audio-visual aids, educational films and educational radio and television broadcasting and, last but not least, research, namely field research on socio-economic aspects of adult education and literacy programmes. If you could supply the Unesco Regional Office with the names and addresses of some of these leading personalities to whom we could write, it would be most helpful.

(ASPBAE Inward Correspondence)

Since early 1960 the international adult education movement had picked up momentum. This could be attributed to the impact of the two major world conferences on adult education. The first was the Unesco World Conference on Adult Education in a Changing World held in Montreal in 1960 and the second was the Unesco World Congress of Ministers of Education on the Eradication of Illiteracy held in Teheran in 1965. The Montreal Conference dealt with the whole field of adult education. Though attention was given to the question of literacy and functional education for adults, many problems related to literacy could not be examined in detail because the scope of the conference agenda was too broad. Moreover, most participants at the Montreal Conference were adult education practitioners who could make recommendations, but they could not commit their governments to the adoption and implementation of such recommendations. On the other hand, the Teheran Conference was attended by ministers of education. Its recommendations were likely to have more immediate influence upon government action because of the level and nature of its official representation.

The majority of the countries represented at Teheran took the congress very seriously because they knew the importance of education, including adult education, to the social and economic development of their countries. Working papers and country reports presented and subsequent discussions sharply revealed the seriousness of the illiteracy situation in the world. Then it was estimated that there were over 700 million illiterate adults in the world and this number was increasing by some 25 million a year through the population explosion. As a regional organization of adult education, ASPBAE was deeply concerned with illiteracy problems and was seriously exploring how it could play a role in helping countries in the Asia and South Pacific region to cope with the problems. It was soon agreed that ASPBAE should continue to organize regional conferences for Asia and the South Pacific along the same lines as the Saigon Conference (1962), Sydney Seminar (1964), and Leverhulme Conference in Hong Kong (1964), which could serve as regional follow-ups to the Teheran Conference enabling the recommendations from Teheran to be examined in greater detail in terms of the special needs and problems of Asia and the South Pacific. The regional seminar on the Role of Educational Institutions in the Promotion of Adult Literacy held in New Delhi in October 1966 was a good example of the bureau's contribution.

In spite of the growing realization among Asian countries of its crucial importance, adult education was still restricted to a marginal position in regard to the national education system. This marginality of adult education resulted from various factors. Modern educational systems in Asia were primarily modelled upon those of the western nations. Compared to the formal education, adult education was introduced to Asia at a much later stage. Immediately after the Second World War several countries in Asia gained their national independence. This was followed by a baby boom in the 1950s which resulted in an overwhelmingly large young population in the newly independent nations and the urgent need of education for the young became the prime concern of the governments. Another important contributing factor to marginality seemed to be the lack of adequate institutional structures and shortage of professionally trained adult education personnel. It was pointed out by de Clerck that 'In too many countries, adult education was taken care of, within the Ministry of Education, by an understaffed Department or Division, with insufficient means and scarce resources' (de Clerck 1968: 15). This miserable state of affairs in adult education prompted Arnold Hely to write a letter to the ministers of education of several Asian countries. His letter dated 29 September 1967 read:

The Asian-South Pacific Bureau of Adult Education is a regional non-government organisation concerned with the promotion and fostering of adult education throughout Asia and the South Pacific area. I enclose some notes which provide a summary of its development, the policy it pursues and the programmes it provides.

The Bureau is concerned with the education of adults. It believes that under today's conditions education must be recognised as a life-long process and that the problems facing the developing countries of Asia and the South Pacific are of such a character and complexity that no formal education in childhood and youth, no matter how thorough, can fit young people to face all the problems they must meet in their maturity. Economic and social development calls for increased concentration upon the 'continuing' education of those who have left school. The fact that in many Asian countries there still remains a problem of mass illiteracy tends to highlight the importance of adult education, since the relationship between illiteracy and a low level of economic and social development is now widely recognised.

However, concern with the problem of organising functional literacy programmes for illiterate adults should not obscure the fact that even if illiteracy was to be eliminated completely, adult education would be more, rather than less important.

The Bureau therefore believes that education must be seen as a life-long integrated process. This means that adult education (including literacy programmes) should be integrated within the framework of the national educational plan. The Bureau also holds that educational planning must be based upon the concept of 'éducation permanente' if it is to be effective, and if wastage of effort and resources are to be eliminated.

(ASPBAE Outward Correspondence)

In November 1967 a conference was held in Singapore and its theme was Urban Adult Education in Developing Countries. Originally proposed by ASPBAE, the conference was jointly organized by the Adult Education Board and the two Departments of Extra-Mural Studies of the University of Singapore and Nanyang University. That was the last conference and executive meeting attended by Arnold Hely because he died suddenly in mid-December 1967 while on a tramping club expedition near Wellington, New Zealand. His death was a great loss to ASPBAE and a bitter blow to his friends and colleagues who had worked with him and knew him well. Indeed he had worked tirelessly and effectively for the establishment and development of ASPBAE. In 1985 when ASPBAE celebrated its twenty-first anniversary in New Delhi, an Arnold Hely Award was established to commemorate his contribution to the bureau.

After the death of Arnold Hely, the bureau almost came to a standstill. However, the ASPBAE Journal, which began in 1964, continued to be published in India under the editorship of Bimla Dutta. Dulcie Stretton of Australia was appointed acting secretary in 1968 and later on Arch Nelson of the University of New England succeeded her in 1971. The first thing that Arch Nelson did was to retrieve all ASPBAE papers and financial reports from Dulcie

Stretton. His priority was to put ASPBAE's financial record straight. In his letter to Des Crowley in March 1972 he wrote

> three things concern me: first, that as an international organization with consultative status with Unesco our books must be in order; second, that though our constitution calls for an annual audit there is no evidence on the file that there has ever been an audit; and, third, that we should be proceeding to raise funds for a dynamic programme and can scarcely do so unless we have our books in order.
>
> (ASPBAE Outward Correspondence)

On these matters alone he spent almost a year. Meanwhile he tried very hard to revive ASPBAE but faced some difficulties. First, his status as secretary had never been confirmed by the chairman. Second, he could neither restore all papers from Dulcie Stretton nor gain access to ASPBAE's remaining funds still kept by her. Third, he was unable to raise funds even for his own travel to attend the Unesco World Conference on Adult Education in Japan 1972. Fourth, there seemed to be some difference in expectations between him and Siva Dutta. The former felt that he would not be able to play an effective role in the bureau unless his status as secretary was confirmed while the latter was trying to appoint someone such as Des Crowley or Chris Duke to be the secretary. Eventually he tendered his resignation to Siva Dutta in September 1972.

During the 'hibernation' of ASPBAE, Siva Dutta, still as its chairman, was able to organize two seminars on the Training of Adult Educators, one in March 1972 and the other in May 1974 both held in New Delhi, India. Apart from these two events, there was hardly any meeting of the ASPBAE executive after the Singapore meeting in November 1967. At best only some members of the bureau's executive committee such as Siva Dutta of India, Arch Nelson of Australia, T.C. Lai of Hong Kong, S. Sangmahli of Thailand, and A.C. Vizconde of the Philippines had been able to meet occasionally at seminars such as those already mentioned.

REDEVELOPMENT OF ASPBAE

Eventually a meeting of some members of the bureau in New Delhi on 7 May 1974 decided that Chris Duke, Director of the Centre for Continuing Education at the Australian National University, should

111

be elected as secretary/treasurer in place of Arch Nelson who had resigned in September 1972. The bureau also decided that a Regional Centre of Continuing Education should be set up at a place outside India, preferably in Kuala Lumpur. Later on as the response from the governments of Thailand, Malaysia, and Singapore was not encouraging for the establishment of a centre in their respective countries, the bureau decided to develop several sub-regional centres in existing adult education organizations and institutions in the following sub-regions:

1 the western part of the region with a centre in Teheran;
2 India as a sub-region rather than just one country, with a centre at New Delhi continuing to produce the journal;
3 the South Pacific region with a centre in Canberra and to be the official business address and headquarters so long as the secretary/treasurer was there;
4 a centre in Ho Chi Minh City to collect information on non-formal education activities in China, Vietnam, Laos, Cambodia, and so on.

On 16 August 1974 Chris Duke wrote to Siva Dutta accepting the position of secretary/treasurer, with copies of the letter to former members of the ASPBAE executive, representatives of several countries in the region, and some well-known adult educators like Roby Kidd of ICAE, P. Bertelsen of Unesco Adult Education Division, and P. Dijkstra of Friedrich-Naumann-Stiftung. In his letter he wrote

Following our recent exchanges of correspondence, since I accepted the position of Secretary-Treasurer, I am writing you an extended letter, copies of which I am also sending to colleagues in several countries in the region. I apologise for doing this, since it might seem to be a discourtesy. However, I am confident that you will appreciate that intention, and the desire to reduce the problems of distance and delay in communication, so that we can breathe more life into the ASPBAE organisation, following your very useful recent Workshop in Delhi, and the proposal arising from that to develop a ASPBAE Regional Centre in Kuala Lumpur.

(ASPBAE Outward Correspondence)

It was obvious that right from the beginning he wished to revive the network of adult educators which Arnold Hely built and which lapsed after his death in 1967. He also wished to rekindle their enthusiasm in and commitment to the adult education movement in the Asian-South Pacific region, and to generate their support for ASPBAE and its proposed Asian-South Pacific Centre for Adult and Continuing Education. Meanwhile he recruited Arch Nelson and Joan Allsop as editors of the *ASPBAE Courier*. In December 1974 the first issue of the *ASPBAE Courier* was launched; in its editorial entitled 'The Redevelopment of ASPBAE', Arch Nelson wrote:

> We intend *ASPBAE Courier* to play an important part in this redevelopment. We are particularly anxious that it should have a wide circulation, and serve to promote the development and exchange of ideas not only among planners and policy makers in the region but, more importantly, among the growing number of working practitioners in the field of adult education. Its focus will be on the ASPBAE Region and we hope that adult educators in the region will help by telling us about their problems, their achievements and their ideas. It will thus be a regional journal, aiming primarily to help regional people to develop their ideas, to put them into practice and to make them known to others.
>
> (*ASPBAE Courier* 1, December 1974: 2)

It was intended that the *Courier* would be published three times a year, in April, August, and December.

During the first two years as secretary/treasurer, Chris Duke visited a number of countries in the region, identified leading adult educators, and built up a network of country contact persons. Then his list of contact persons included Sman Sangmahli and Kowit Vorapipatana of Thailand, Jong-Gon Hwang of Korea, T.C. Lai of Hong Kong, Joe Conceicao of Singapore, Kinichi Komada of Japan, W.M.K. Wijetunga of Sri Lanka, Anwas Iskandar of Indonesia, and David James of New Zealand.

In June 1976 the ICAE organized and held a major international conference on Adult Education and Development in Dar es Salaam, Tanzania. With the encouragement and moral support of Roby Kidd, Secretary-General of ICAE, and a generous grant of US$12,000 from ICAE, Chris Duke was able to invite a strong contingent of Asian delegates for the ICAE conference and the ASPBAE executive meeting. The meeting discussed and revised the constitution to make it more adapted to the practical problems of communication and management of this large regional organization. It was decided that the whole ASPBAE region should be reorganized into four sub-regions, with Region 1 being South Asia, Region 2 being China and her communist neighbours, Region 3 being South-East and East Asia including Australia, and Region 4 being Pacific Island countries and New Zealand.

At the same conference in Dar es Salaam, an Asian Region Working Group was formed to look into the problems and needs in adult education in Asia. The working group concentrated their examination and discussion on sub-region 3, the most diverse of the Asian sub-regions, from those which are mostly rural to those which are entirely urbanized. The group eventually identified some urgent needs for the development of adult education in the sub-region, such as the training of adult educators, development of reading materials for new literates, programme evaluation procedures and improvements of the quality of adult education programmes, and the need for adult education structures. The group also considered what action could be taken in the next three years through the sub-regional mechanism of ASPBAE. In this respect, they suggested

1 that an inventory of innovative programmes in adult education available in each country should be drawn up;
2 that ASPBAE should encourage the formation of national associations of adult education in its member countries;
3 that ASPBAE should promote inter-country visits to innovative projects;
4 that ASPBAE should organize a number of short training workshops for adult educators;
5 that ASPBAE should conduct a workshop on the implications of urbanization for adult education; and
6 that ASPBAE should plan training for the use of mass media for adult educators.

(ASPBAE 1976 *Report*: 1–2)

Since late 1973 Bernd Pflug of DVV had been discussing with Chris Duke the possibility of German support for ASPBAE. Just two months before the ICAE Conference in Dar es Salaam, Bernd Pflug sent a piece of good news to Chris Duke. In his letter of April 1976, he wrote:

During these months, we prepare a plan to extend our educational aid programme to Asia from 1978 onwards. The Ministry of Economic Cooperation intends to increase the budget of this DVV-department slightly but steadily in the following years. Besides a programme in the Indian region . . . we should like to cooperate with ASPBAE as the major regional adult education association. According to our preliminary estimation, a yearly contribution of DM100,000 that is nowadays roughly US$35,000 might be possible for ASPBAE activities.

(ASPBAE Inward Correspondence)

Although the matter had not yet been confirmed, Bernd Pflug suggested that Chris Duke should hold preliminary discussions on programme possibilities during the ASPBAE executive meeting in Dar es Salaam in June 1976. He also advised him on both the format and content of programme proposals. Finally he recommended that ASPBAE should plan a workshop for the second half of 1977 to discuss programme proposals in detail. This good news was indeed a positive turning-point in Chris Duke's efforts to redevelop ASPBAE.

The proposed workshop entitled ASPBAE Region 3 Programmatic Workshop was held in Chiangmai, northern Thailand, 21–28 November 1977. Participants came from Australia, Hong Kong, Indonesia, Malaysia, Philippines, Singapore, South Korea, and Thailand. In addition there were observers from the South-East Asian Ministers of Education Organization (SEAMEO), the National Education Council, the Ministry of Education and the Adult Education Division, and five universities of Thailand. Siva Dutta and Kowit Vorapipatana served as resource persons. It was the most important ASPBAE Conference since the Sydney Seminar of 1964. If the Sydney Seminar were to mark the birth of ASPBAE, then this Programmatic Workshop would symbolize its reincarnation. As a result of this workshop, many programme proposals together with their budget estimates were drafted and later submitted to DVV for consideration. Eventually, based on these proposals, DVV provided the first triennial support for the period 1978–80. Since then ASPBAE and DVV have entered a mode of partnership in the development of adult education in the Asian-South Pacific region and later on the DVV triennial support was renewed for the further periods 1981–3, 1984–6, and 1987–9.

Expressing his gratitude to DVV for its generous support, Chris Duke wrote:

> Much credit is due to the professional tenacity and openmindedness of the DVV officers especially responsible for developing this partnership – Bernd Pflug initially . . . ; then Heribert Hinzen; and more recently Wolfgang Leumer, support throughout by the head of DVV's international branch, Jakob Horn.
>
> (Duke 1985: 18)

The programme proposals for the initial triennium (1978–80) requested an estimated budget of US$257,500 to cover expenses of three main items – training workshops, publications, and travelling fellowships. Over the years, the bureau's budget has gradually increased. The present budget for the period 1987–9 amounts to more than 1 million US dollars. The expenditure items have also been expanded to include the courier service, troubleshooter, research and evaluation and administration of programmes in addition to those already mentioned. In recent years the bureau usually receives more programme proposals from country members than it can cope with from DVV funds. Though attempts have been made to secure other sources of funding, they have not been successful. Initially Chris Duke tried to seek partnership with the Dutch Folkhighschool Association (VVV), in addition to the ASPBAE–DVV partnership, but his attempts eventually fell through.

The success of the Programmatic Workshop encouraged Chris Duke to organize more annual conferences in different countries of ASPBAE Region 3: the Philippines in 1978, South Korea in 1979, and Indonesia in 1980. Since then these conferences have been held biennially, in Japan (1982), Malaysia (1984), and Macau (1986). The next conference will be held in Singapore in 1988. Through these conferences Chris Duke had been able to consolidate and strengthen the network of adult educators and national associations which he had built over the years. Several national associations of adult education had been formed, mainly as a result of his encouragement and guidance. These conferences had provided opportunities not only for adult educators to interact among themselves and exchange ideas and experiences, but also for the bureau to review its past activities, redefine directions, and set priorities for future programmes.

In February 1978 ASPBAE in association with the South Pacific Commission organized a Regional Planning Conference on Adult Education in National Development. Held at Noumea, New Caledonia, the conference brought together representatives of eleven Pacific governments and nine regional and international organizations to determine priority needs and strategies for the development of adult and non-formal education in participating countries and to consider means by which national efforts in this direction could be strengthened through regional co-operation and mutual assistance. Many recommendations were made and some were addressed to ASPBAE, strongly advocating the setting up of ASPBAE Region 4 to cover all countries and territories in the South Pacific including New Zealand. The conference also identified various tasks for the newly proposed Region 4, such as preparation of a directory of adult education organizations, a regional ASPBAE newsletter and an inventory of resource persons, development of national associations, organization of regional conferences and training workshops, and the establishment of an ASPBAE scholarship fund. On the last day of the conference, while the conference was temporarily adjourned, a separate meeting of ASPBAE was held. The meeting formally proposed the establishment of ASPBAE Region 4 and decided that the office of the new region should be located in Suva, the capital of Fiji. Manasa Lasaro of the Pacific Theological College was elected chairman of the first executive committee. Though there was much excitement and enthusiasm among members at the formation of the ASPBAE Region 4, there was hardly any follow-up activity. However, in Fiji Manasa Lasaro managed to conduct a series of training programmes throughout the country. The Region 4 executive committee had not been able to meet at regular intervals mainly because of the great distance that separates one island state from the other, transport problems, and lack of resources.

By the end of the first triennium (1978–80) the bureau had already achieved most of the objectives which it formulated at the Chiangmai Programmatic Workshop in November 1977. It had made significant contributions to the development of adult education in the following areas:

1 encouragement and assistance in the formation and strengthening of national associations of adult education in several member countries;

2 building up a regional network of adult educators and organizations through regional activities and personal influence of the secretary-general;
3 assistance in regional and national training programmes and conferences of member countries;
4 provision of opportunities for adult educators to continue their professional growth through Travelling Fellowships and Kellogg Fellowships and Scholarships;
5 co-operation with other regional and international organizations such as DVV, Unesco Regional Office for Education in Asia and Oceania, ICAE, SEAMEO, ILO, CIDA, and the South Pacific Commission;
6 establishment of a very effective and efficient clearing-house on adult education through the Courier Service;
7 assistance in the translation, production, and distribution of learning materials in some member countries.

These achievements of the bureau should be attributed to the tremendous drive and leadership of Chris Duke and the active support of his assistant, Yvonne Heslop. At that time Chris Duke was holding three responsible positions: Director of the Centre for Continuing Education at the Australian National University, Secretary-General of ASPBAE, and Associate Secretary-General of ICAE. Since ASPBAE has been regarded as a regional arm of ICAE, his positions in both organizations provided a very close working relationship to the two partners in adult education. In mid-1980 he and Roby Kidd visited the People's Republic of China. The major outcomes of the visit were a study visit to China by an international team of adult educators in 1981 and an international adult education symposium in Shanghai in May 1984. The latter was seen as a starting-point for further bilateral linkages between China and other countries in the field of adult education.

At the bureau's executive meeting in Hong Kong in October 1983, the secretary-general reviewed some principles and questions of importance in taking a long-term view of the role of ASPBAE, which included the following:

1 The special professional character of ASPBAE with its combination of non-government and government members.
2 Who benefits from its work – do the benefits reach those most in need?

3 Who takes part in its planning and other activities – is the network widening?

4 Are there new kinds of activities to be undertaken (in addition to workshops and training courses, travelling fellowships, publications, translation, and research)?

5 What subject areas have in the past been identified as important but not taken up (e.g. linkage of formal and non-formal education, traditional culture, adult education for women)?

6 Are there new subject areas that should now be considered?

7 What about the use of languages other than English for teaching, publication, and so on?

8 What about the relationship with ICAE and its various programmes and activities?

9 Does the present regional structure strike the right balance between separate sub-regions and wider exchanges?

10 Can the secretariat responsibilities be further devolved from Canberra?

(ASPBAE *Courier Service – News* 29, December 1983: 2)

After a lengthy discussion, it was resolved that all member countries should send indications of their needs for training and other professional adult education development matters for the next five years for consideration and that ASPBAE should take stock of resources and examine how these could be matched with needs.

In the 1980s there has been rapid economic growth in Asia, particularly in the newly industrialized countries (NICs) and territories, such as Hong Kong, Singapore, South Korea, and Taiwan. Two main factors attributed to the rapid economic growth of NICs are: first, the high educational standards of the people, and second, the easy transfer of technology from highly developed countries to NICs mainly through the multinational corporations and governmental efforts. As the NICs forsake conventional skills of production and move into higher technology, a large section of the labour force finds their skills obsolete. Consequently this rapid change of technology has led to a massive retraining of workers and drastic change in their living and working conditions. In adult education greater emphasis has been placed on basic technical and vocational training, health and environmental education, computer and information systems, management and communication skills, and law. While the NICs are moving into higher technology, some countries in the region are still economically backward. Larger parts of their population are still

119

farmers, living off land, river, and sea. The major problems confronting these countries are rural poverty and illiteracy. Therefore the provision of training programmes for income-generating and literacy programmes has been the main concerns of adult education. The impact of technology and mass media on the rural people has intensified in recent years. It is generally agreed among adult educators in the region that the introduction of technology in rural areas must be 'appropriate'; otherwise it may do more harm than good to the people.

Due to different rates and stages of economic development, each country has its own peculiar needs and problems. Even within a country itself there are disparities between urban cities and rural areas. Therefore a systematic approach should be adopted in programme planning, taking into consideration various kinds of local and national needs, so that adult education programmes are planned on the bases of well-defined objectives and in line with the national developmental goals of each country. At the Region 1 executive meeting in New Delhi in September 1985, members were urged to adopt this approach when they put up programme proposals seeking financial support. Some national associations of NICs were also encouraged to be more self-reliant and, if possible, share their resources with their counterparts in poorer countries. Member countries like Australia, New Zealand, and Japan are prohibited from using DVV funds for their own activities. However, they have contributed much to ASPBAE, particularly Australia, in terms of leadership and resources. For some years Singapore has been self-supporting in national programmes and able to assist in some way in the organization of regional training programmes and other activities of the bureau. It is hoped that Hong Kong and South Korea will be able to do likewise in the near future.

During a Think Tank Meeting in Singapore in May 1983, there were discussions on the 'possibility of moving the Secretariat [from Canberra] to Singapore in order to make it closer to Asia and make it more Asian' (Leumer 1983: 16). This idea was actually originated by Chris Duke who believed that the secretariat should not be located in one country or region for too long a period and that the position of the secretary-general should be rotated among leading adult educators in the entire Asian and South Pacific region. But at that time, there was hardly anyone in Singapore or elsewhere in the region ready to take over the position of the secretary-general. It is an honorary position which carries numerous tasks and heavy responsibilities. Only people with altruism and strong commitment to adult education, like Arnold Hely, Helmuth Dolff, Roby Kidd, and Chris Duke, are willing to take up such a challenge. Furthermore, the bureau has no assets and infrastructure, and no salaried staff. Since 1974 it had depended heavily on the Centre for Continuing Education of ANU for support in terms of manpower, facilities, and resources. No other universities in Asia are so supportive of adult education and can afford to be so generous and broadminded as ANU. Eventually it was decided that the administration of the bureau should be gradually decentralized. As a start two regional offices were formed in early 1984 – Region 1 Office in Colombo, Sri Lanka, and Region 3 Office in Singapore – each being entrusted with the management of funds and programmes that have direct contractual arrangements with DVV.

PRESENT POSITION AND PROSPECTS

In June 1985 Chris Duke resigned his position as secretary-general and left Australia for the UK to take up an appointment as Professor of Continuing and Adult Education at the University of Warwick. His departure from the region was indeed a sorrowful event for his colleagues who had appreciated his dedication and contributions to the development of adult education in Asia and the South Pacific. To keep the bureau going, W.M.K. Wijetunga of Region 1 Office was soon selected to be the new secretary-general. In appreciation of Chris Duke's contribution to ASPBAE, Wijetunga wrote:

Chris Duke served ASPBAE, as its Secretary-General, for the longest period, of nearly twelve years. In the twenty-one years of ASPBAE, it reached its highest water-mark during the able and dynamic stewardship of Chris Duke. His own Centre in Canberra was like a melting pot, to which he brought, using the Centre's resources, resources of the Australian government, and those of cooperating international agencies, adult educators, both young and old, and men and women from all over Asia and the Pacific. They came from both better known places in Asia, as well as those least known to many. However they came year after year, to learn and unlearn, to act and interact, in the democratic and egalitarian atmosphere, created and nourished

121

by the Centre and its curious mix of academics. The Centre was no doubt used by Chris Duke, with no reservations and inhibitions to build and consolidate ASPBAE. So much so that before long CCE and Chris Duke became synonymous with ASPBAE.

(Wijetunga 1985: 25)

The change of leadership had accelerated the pace of the bureau's decentralization. With his office in Colombo, Wijetunga took over most of the administrative responsibilities of the secretariat except some financial matters and the production of the *Courier Service*. His position as the new secretary-general was confirmed at the executive meeting held in New Delhi in September 1985. Lim Hoy Pick was elected as chairman of Region 3 for a further term and Ananda Jayawardana of Sri Lanka became the secretary for Region 1, a position formerly held by Wijetunga. Yvonne Heslop was appointed as executive co-ordinator with responsibility for looking after the affairs of Regions 2 and 4; she would also continue as editor of the ASPBAE *Courier Service*. For a number of years she has been doing an excellent job in editing and producing the *Courier Service* at regular intervals. By December 1986 a total of thirty-eight issues of *Courier Service – News*, seventeen issues of *Newsletter*, thirty-eight issues of *Learning Exchange*, and thirty-eight issues of *ASPBAE Courier* (a collection of articles or country reports on adult education) had been produced and distributed to all members of the bureau.

The executive meeting at New Delhi discussed a number of issues, including the bureau's constitution. There was a proposal to form an advisory council of ASPBAE with memberships drawn from some older members who had made outstanding contributions to the bureau. Since there was no provision in the constitution for the advisory council, amendments to the constitution were therefore necessary in order to incorporate such a provision. A.T. Ariyaratne, president of ASPBAE and chairman of the meeting, agreed to redraft the constitution and table it for discussion at the next meeting. Other matters discussed and decided at the meeting were as follows:

It was decided . . . that ASPBAE would develop a new set of guidelines for its programmes, particularly in readiness for a new triennium of funding through the German Adult Education

Association (DVV) from 1987–1989. Since a great deal of the ground work has now been laid in Asia, programmes can take on a more integrated aspect, and with the good news that funding would be forthcoming forward planning will be undertaken in a more systematic way than in the past. It was further decided to give particular emphasis to developing programmes and networks in the Pacific region in the coming years, and also to developing closer links with colleagues in China.

(ASPBAE *Courier Service – News* 35, December 1985: 3)

Accordingly Wijetunga developed a new set of guidelines for the submission of programme proposals and sent it to national associations and contact persons of member countries in January 1986. In the guidelines he also gave an account of the present status and new aspirations of the bureau:

ASPBAE relies heavily on other institutions for support, as well as for resources, and on the voluntary, unpaid, time of adult educators throughout the region. This has advantages and disadvantages for ASPBAE's mode of operation, but does provide considerable flexibility to respond to changing needs and circumstances not available to more bureaucratised organisations.

The ASPBAE network is now well established throughout Asia, and increasingly the Pacific, with most countries in the region taking part in at least some activities. Development of this network through means of travelling fellowships and professional problem-solving sectors of the programme could be encouraged in the coming three years. Exchange of experience and expertise could be built into the programmes of member organizations. Such exchange over the past few years has reinforced the distinctive features of adult education in member countries and has acted as protection against a sense of inferiority and a tendency to import unsuitable foreign models . . . .

ASPBAE emphasises technical cooperation between developing countries for sharing and mutual help. This does not exclude western experts and experience but puts priority on interpersonal and inter-country teamwork. Small scale programmes are preferred to massive approaches. Adult education in the context of development rather than an end in itself is another key emphasis of ASPBAE. The word 'development' is used in the broad and humane sense embracing social and cultural matters rather than merely economic progress. ASPBAE also values the purposes and approaches referred to as 'conscientisation' as a means of raising awareness among the poor and underprivileged in countries of the region.

(ASPBAE *Newsletter* 16, May 1986: 2)

At the Region 3 executive meeting held in Macau in November 1986, some questions arising from the constitution were again brought up for discussion. Two major issues were identified: the membership and the structure of ASPBAE, both of which, if resolved, might require further amendments to the constitution. On the question of membership, some members in favour of multiple country memberships argued that with wider range of participation and contribution, ASPBAE would be strengthened, and that in some countries governments played a major providing role, alongside a non-governmental national association. Those who opposed the idea argued that multiple country memberships would create unhealthy rivalry among different organizations and animosity among adult educators within a country. Since the views of Region 1 would also be sought on this matter, it was decided that a survey would be carried out by the secretary-general to seek the views of all ASPBAE country members. As for structure, it was suggested that the three vice-presidents of ICAE representing Asia and the Pacific should be invited to sit on the ASPBAE executive to serve as a link between ASPBAE and ICAE, as Chris Duke did when he was associate secretary-general of ICAE. Therefore the ASPBAE executive would be made up of eleven members, comprising four regional chairpersons, three vice-presidents of ICAE, and four nominees of the sub-regional executives. It was also suggested that the bureau should have a Programme Advisory Committee to assist in the development of programmes. Finally the meeting discussed whether Regions 2 and 3 should regroup according to a suggestion that Region 2 should be enlarged to embrace China, Japan, Korea, Taiwan, Macau, and Hong Kong, while Region 3 should cover Australia and all the countries in South-East Asia. So far no decisions have been taken on these matters. All the suggestions will be carried out only after they have been accepted by the majority of members and necessary amendments to the constitution have been made.

Under the present leadership of Wijetunga, the bureau's

activities have picked up momentum and programmes for 1987 are being implemented according to schedule. He has just retired from his university, so he will be devoting more time to ASPBAE. He will be travelling more often to member countries for consultations and reinforcement of the bureau's network. Through regular correspondence, he keeps up with DVV, the executive co-ordinator, chairman of Region 3, and contact persons who are responsible for ASPBAE-sponsored programmes. With his strong commitment to adult education in general and dedication to the work of ASPBAE in particular, there is no doubt that ASPBAE will continue to grow and gain more general acceptance by countries in the Asian and South Pacific region.

REFERENCES

ASPBAE *Annual Reports*, 1964–1966.
ASPBAE *ASPBAE Courier*, 1–4, 19–38.
ASPBAE *Courier Service – News*, 19–38.
ASPBAE *Newsletter* 2–17.
ASPBAE *Learning Exchange*, 19–38.
ASPBAE *Minutes of the Executive Meetings*, 1964–1967, 1977–1986.
ASPBAE *Inward Correspondence*, 1966–1967.
ASPBAE *General Correspondence*, 1970–1976.
ASPBAE *Outward Correspondence*, 1967–1968.
ASPBAE (1976) *Extract from: Report from the Asian Region Working Party of the ICAE Conference on Adult Education and Development, Dar es Salaam, June 1976.*
ASPBAE *Reports to DVV*, 1983–1986.
Clerck, M. de (1968) *Adult Education for a Changing World*, unpublished paper dated October 1968.
Duke, C. (1985) 'ASPBAE second phase – new modes of partnership 1974–85', in S.C. Dutta (ed.) *ASPBAE Comes of Age 1964–85*, Canberra: ASPBAE.
Dutta, S.C. (1974) *ASPBAE Centre for Continuing Education: Report of a Workshop held in Delhi, May 1974*, New Delhi: ASPBAE.
Dutta, S.C. and Fischer, H.J. (1972) *Training of Adult Educators: Proceedings of a Seminar held in New Delhi, March 1972*, Bombay: ASPBAE and Friedrich Naumann Stiftung.
Hely, A. (1964) *Report on the Leverhulme Conference on 'South-East Asian Universities and Extramural Studies'*, dated 2 December 1964.
—— (1966) *Report on the UNESCO World Congress of Ministers of Education on the Eradication of Illiteracy held at Teheran in 1965, with Special Reference to Its Relevance to Asian Conditions*, dated 1 October 1966.
Leumer, W. (1983) 'Asia is different', *Courier Service – News* 29, December.

South Pacific Commission (1978) *Regional Planning Conference on Adult Education in National Development: Report of a Meeting held in Noumea, in February 1978*.

Wijetunga, W.M.K. (1985) 'ASPBAE – 21 years later', in S.C. Dutta (ed.) *ASPBAE Comes of Age 1964–85*, Canberra: ASPBAE.

9

The Caribbean Regional Council for Adult Education: its scope, directions, and achievements

Esmond Ramesar

INTRODUCTION

The Caribbean area consists of the archipelago of islands stretching from the Bahamas in the north to Trinidad and Tobago in the south; the mainland countries of Guyana, Suriname, and Guyane (Cayenne) on the South American continent; Belize in Central America; and Curaçao and Aruba off the northern coast of South America.

The area is made up of territories with a relatively long history of independence (Haiti became independent in 1804) to territories which have only recently achieved nationhood (Antigua and Barbuda became independent in 1981). Their populations vary from as many as 10 million in Cuba to 10,000 in the British Virgin Islands. Their language, culture, and education reflect their colonial past. For example, the language, culture, and education in Cuba, Santo Domingo, and Puerto Rico reflect a Spanish past; in the Commonwealth Caribbean an English past is reflected; Haiti, Martinique, Guadeloupe, and Guyane have a French past; and in Netherlands Antilles and Suriname it is a Dutch past that is reflected. There are also pockets of original, native people in Guyana and in Belize.

The ethnic composition of the area is equally varied – from the descendants of Dutch settlers in the Netherlands Windwards to descendants of African slaves in Haiti; mulattos in Santo Domingo; large proportions of descendants of immigrants from India in Suriname; (60 per cent), Guyana (55 per cent), and Trinidad and Tobago (45 per cent); Indonesians in Suriname; and Chinese and Arabs in most countries. Ideologically there is also variety – from the Marxist Socialist Left of Cuba to the Liberal Democratic Right of Barbados. In economic terms there is a disparity of wealth from the relatively high per capita income of US$4,000 (Trinidad and Tobago) to the relatively low per capita income of US$150 (Haiti). The keynote is diversity, and adult education in the Caribbean reflects all these many and varied backgrounds.

CARIBBEAN ADULT EDUCATION IN THE WORLD CONTEXT

Adult education is not a new activity in the Caribbean. Attempts were made during the late colonial period to provide literacy classes for adults. It is for this reason that the use of the phrase 'adult education' is problematical in the Caribbean context. To the minds of many – and this includes important decision-makers – adult education is either perceived as literacy classes or as a very marginal operation. Perhaps we of the faith have done a poor job in convincing our governments and public at large that adult education is more, that it is

the provision of learning experience and activities, other than those provided in the formal education system, for persons who are participants in the processes of society;

that its aim is

to enhance the individual's quality of life and to enable him/her to contribute more effectively to the development of society;

that as a consequence teachers of adults

are all those persons in society who are actively involved as facilitators in the process described above, e.g. Agricultural Extension Officers, Paramedics, Family Life Educators, Community Development Officers, Media Personnel, etc.

National (territorial) governments in the Caribbean have accepted these definitions, but in typical fashion they have not acted on them, in making the necessary organizational, administrative, and financial provision.

UNESCO'S INVOLVEMENT IN ADULT EDUCATION

Very early after the founding of the United Nations, its economic, social, and cultural arm – Unesco – recognized adult education as an area of activity which deserved attention. As a consequence a conference on the subject was held in 1949 followed by others at convenient periods.

The First International Conference on Adult Education (Unesco) was held in Elsinore, Denmark, in 1949; Elsinore was chosen as the venue because Denmark was among the leading countries which gave adult education its modern thrust. Because it was 1949 when leadership in world affairs was essentially Eurocentric, the conference was dominated by delegates from twenty-nine western Europe countries and North America. It was not surprising that the conference adopted a relatively narrow view of the functions of adult education, that is the role of liberal and vocational education, and stressing the important role of voluntary organizations as opposed to government involvement.

The Second International Conference on Adult Education was held in Montreal, Canada, in 1960. At this conference there was representation from fifty-one countries with a substantial proportion from the non-industrialized world. It was no wonder that this expanded representation saw fit to go beyond the narrow confines of the previous conference and revised the functions of adult education to include any organized attempt to offer education to adults no matter what its level or purpose.

It was at this conference that the principle of lifelong education was reiterated and promulgated as the goal for future policies of governments. In fact the Final Report explicitly charged:

Nothing less will suffice than that people everywhere should come to accept adult education as a normal and as a necessary part of the educational provision of every country.

The impetus of the Montreal Conference gave rise to enormous and wide participation in adult education activities in many countries.

Twelve years after Montreal, the Third International Conference on Adult Education was held in Tokyo, Japan, in 1972

1   to examine the trends in adult education during the preceding decade;
2   to consider the future of adult education in the context of lifelong learning; and
3   to review the strategies of educational development in respect of adult education.

It was significant that this conference was held in a non-Eurocentric country. There were over 400 delegates from 82 countries with a majority coming from the non-industrialized world. At Elsinore it was a meeting of minds of adult education practitioners. At Montreal the majority was from among professional/academic adult educators. At Tokyo, the majority of delegates consisted of educational administrators and politicians with responsibility for determining and executing educational policy.

Although many themes were discussed, the dominant motif of the conference was a concern for the education of the disadvantaged with the observation that the overwhelming majority of each country's population was not participating in adult education, and that this same majority mainly comprised the socially and economically handicapped. The Final Report emphasized this concern:

> Experience shows that the provision of more education in most communities tends to favour most the already well-educated; the educationally underprivileged have yet to claim their rights. Adult education is no exception to the rule, for those adults who most need education have been largely neglected – they are the forgotten people. Thus the major task of adult education during the Second Development Decade of the United Nations is to seek out and serve those forgotten people.

The Fourth International Conference was held in Paris in 1985.

EARLY BEGINNINGS IN CARIBBEAN ADULT EDUCATION

While the above activities were taking place internationally, parallel activities were taking place in the Caribbean.

The First Regional Conference on Adult Education took place in Jamaica in 1952. It was not surprising that much of what was discussed at this conference related to adult education and social work or community development, because adult education as a discipline in its own right had not yet gained respectability. Later, in 1957, the Adult Education Association of Guyana was established.

The Second Regional Conference on Adult Education was held in Guyana in 1970. A major contributor to that conference was J.

Roby Kidd on the Needs and Objectives of Adult Education. In his closing remarks he shared with others his very insightful perceptions of the Caribbean, and it is a matter worthy of note that the region is still awakening to the potential which Roby Kidd long ago clearly sensed:

> The people of the Caribbean still need to know themselves and to prove themselves, as most peoples everywhere need to do. But increasingly, they will need and they will find the courage and confidence, to be themselves. And when they do, who can tell what will be the contribution of such a people to the world beyond the sea!

What came out of the conference was that there should be more co-operation between adult educators in the Caribbean, since the number of adult education practitioners was quite noticeable as adult education was becoming more defined.

Perhaps the most important adult education event to have taken place in the Caribbean was the Third Regional Conference on Adult Education held in St Lucia in 1977 on the theme Realities and Aspirations in Adult Education in the Context of the Caribbean. This conference was mounted by the CARICOM Secretariat with a grant from the Commonwealth Fund for Technical Co-operation (CFTC). For Caribbean adult educators, this conference represented a watershed in the history of adult education because of the subsequent events which have taken place.

The Fourth Regional Conference was sponsored by the Government of St Lucia and the Unesco regional office in Latin America and the Caribbean, and held in St Lucia in 1980. It was a meeting of experts from adult education institutions in the Caribbean. The theme of this conference was New Emphases for Adult Education in the Caribbean for the Eighties. It was not surprising that the conference confirmed many of the recommendations of the Third Regional Conference.

THE CARIBBEAN REGIONAL COUNCIL FOR ADULT EDUCATION (CARCAE)

It would appear that the Caribbean Regional Council for Adult Education (CARCAE) was formed by a confluence of two separate and independent sets of circumstances:

1 those originating through the International Council for Adult Education;
2 the recommendation of the Seminar/Workshop on Adult Education in the Caribbean sponsored by the Caribbean Community Secretariat (CARICOM), held in Castries, St Lucia, 12–17 May 1977.

At the 1976 ICAE general assembly held in Dar es Salaam, at which Caribbean representatives were present, the point was made that the Caribbean – and more specifically the English-speaking Caribbean – when involved in the Latin American Region, was at a disadvantage because of its size and cultural history. The suggestion was accepted that discussion should take place with the view to giving consideration to the establishment of the English-speaking Caribbean as a sub-region within the Latin American region.

In the following year the CARICOM secretariat held its seminar/workshop on adult education in Castries (May 1977) and made the recommendation that a regional commission should be established to co-ordinate adult education activities within the region. This recommendation was later accepted by the standing committee of ministers of education at its meeting held in 1978.

During the same year (1977) at the ICAE executive meeting held in Delhi, discussion on the Dar es Salaam suggestion that the English-speaking Caribbean should be recognized as a sub-region within the Latin American region continued. This led to the general consensus that something should be done, bearing in mind the peculiar circumstances of the English-speaking Caribbean.

Again during 1977, and following the attendance at the US Adult Education (AEA) general assembly in Detroit, and aware of the discussion which had taken place at the 1977 ICAE executive meeting in Delhi, Samuel Small, Leonard Shorey, and Esmond Ramesar were invited to the ICAE headquarters in Toronto to discuss development in adult education in the Caribbean.

It was reported to the ICAE secretary-general that the CARICOM Conference on Adult Education (1977) made, among others, two significant recommendations about region-wide adult education:

1 that a Commission for Adult Education should be established;
2 that the training of adult educators within the region should be viewed as a matter of priority.

The ICAE, through its secretary-general, immediately agreed, and took the initiative by setting up an interim council, the Caribbean Regional Council for Adult Education (CARCAE), to oversee the promotion of

1 the formation of national/territorial organizations/associations on adult education;
2 a permanent Regional Council for Adult Education by the holding of a general assembly of members and potential members;
3 the drafting of a constitution for the Regional Council;
4 the representation of CARCAE at regional and international meetings;
5 the mounting of a course for adult educators.

With reference to the mounting of the course for adult educators, the ICAE agreed to provide CAN$10,000 for each year of the first cycle of the course, as a tangible support of its concern.

In 1978 at the ICAE executive meeting held in San José, Costa Rica, the decision was taken to recognize the Caribbean not as a sub-region within the Latin American region, but as a region in its own right to represent all the non-Spanish-speaking Caribbean, that is the Dutch/English/French-speaking countries.

At the ICAE general assembly held in Helsinki (1979), the non-Spanish-speaking Caribbean was given full recognition as a region in its own right through the election of Dr Kurleigh King (then secretary-general of CARICOM) as vice-president of ICAE from the Caribbean, and Esmond Ramesar as a member of the executive of ICAE, representing CARCAE.

SUBSEQUENT DEVELOPMENTS

The interim council of CARCAE was set up in 1978 consisting of the following foundation members:

Leonard Shorey, extra-mural tutor, University of the West Indies, Barbados – chairman
Esmond Ramesar, tutor for extra-mural studies, University of the West Indies, Trinidad – executive secretary
Patricia Charles, resident tutor for St Lucia, University of the West Indies, St Lucia – executive member

Louis Profitt, secretary of the Adult Education Association of Guyana – executive member
Samuel Small, co-ordinator of extra-mural studies, University of Guyana, Guyana – executive member.

The preparation of professional adult educators

The committee saw the mounting of a three-year post-graduate certificate course for adult educators as one of the first important activities of CARCAE as evidence of its seriousness in promoting adult education in the Caribbean. The course was mounted by the Extra-Mural Studies Unit, University of the West Indies (UWI), St Augustine (Trinidad) Campus; in association with the Department of Extra-Mural Studies, University of Guyana (UG), Turkeyen (Guyana) Campus; under the aegis of the International Council for Adult Education (ICAE). It was planned that the course would be done over three vacation (summer) periods.

The course outline for the first two cycles (Cycle I and Cycle II) was as follows

Year One/Introductory/First Year

1.1 Language Skills and Communication (c)	37.5 contact hours
1.2 Community Adult Education and Development (c)	37.5 contact hours
1.3 The History of Adult Education in the Caribbean (o)	37.5 contact hours
OR Group Dynamics in Adult Education (o)	37.5 contact hours

First intersessional period: minor term paper of a descriptive nature on an adult education topic (3,500–5,000 words).

Year Two/Intermediate/Second Year

2.1 The Maturation Process in Adult Education (c)	37.5 contact hours
2.2 Research Methods in Adult Education (c)	37.5 contact hours
2.3 Labour Education and Co-operatives (o)	37.5 contact hours
OR Family Life Education (o)	37.5 contact hours

Second intersessional period: major term paper of a more serious nature on an adult education topic based on research carried out by participant (7,500–10,000 words).

Year Three/Final/Third Year

3.1	Methods and Techniques in Adult Education (c)	37.5 contact hours
3.2	Planning and Administration in Adult Education (c)	37.5 contact hours
3.3	Adult Education and Youth Leadership (o)	37.5 contact hours
OR	Guidance and Counselling in Adult Education (o)	37.5 contact hours

(c) = core subject   (o) = optional subject

The number of people completing Cycle I in 1980 was twenty five, of whom fourteen were from the Caribbean Overseas and eleven were from Trinidad and Tobago. The second cycle (Cycle II) began in 1981 and ended in 1983 when twenty one people graduated, with thirteen coming from the Caribbean Overseas.

The year 1984 was a rest period when an evaluation of Cycles I and II was undertaken through a grant from the German Adult Education Association (DVV). As a result of the evaluation exercise the following course structure emerged.

Year One/Introductory/First Year

1.1	History and Philosophy of Adult Education (c)	37.5 contact hours
1.2	The Maturation Process and Adult Education (c)	37.5 contact hours
1.3	Community Adult Education and Development (c)	37.5 contact hours

Minor intersessional paper: 3,500–5,000 words

Year Two/Intermediate/Second Year

2.1	Programme Planning and Evaluation in Adult Education (c)	37.5 contact hours
2.2	Research Methods in Adult Education (c)	37.5 contact hours

2.3 Methods and Techniques in Adult Education (Teachers) (a)	37.5 contact hours
OR Programme Administration and Management in Adult Education (Planners/Administrators) (a)	37.5 contact hours

Major intersessional paper: 7,500–10,000 words

Year Three/Final/Third Year

3.1 Training Methodologies in Adult Education (c)	37.5 contact hours
3.2 Group Dynamics in Adult Education (Teachers) (a)	37.5 contact hours
OR Case Studies in Adult Education (Planners/Administrators) (a)	37.5 contact hours
3.3 Curriculum Development: Materials Production in Adult Education (Planners/Administrators)(a)	37.5 contact hours
OR Delivery Systems in Adult Education (Planners/Administrators) (a)	37.5 contact hours
OR Training in Literacy Methods and Techniques (Teachers) (a)	37.5 contact hours

(c) = core subject   (a) = alternative subject

Twenty-one people are expected to complete the third cycle (Cycle III) in August 1987.

Partial scholarships have been provided by the German Adult Education Association (DVV) for some Caribbean Overseas participants for Cycles II and III. Similar provisions were made by the Canadian International Development Agency (CIDA), and Unesco in respect of Cycle I.

Fourth Caribbean Regional Conference on Adult Education

This Conference/Seminar on Adult Education was held in Castries, St Lucia, and sponsored jointly by the St Lucian Government and Unesco Regional Education Office for Latin America and the Caribbean (ORELAC) in September 1980 when the theme New Emphases for Adult Education in the Caribbean in the Eighties was discussed. Among the many recommendations in the final report of the meeting the following are of special interest:

1 that the UWI Extra-Mural Studies Unit's Library on Adult Education be assisted in developing further its resources and in providing the library services necessary to adult education organizations throughout the region;
2 that a Communications Centre be established for the purpose of servicing adult education institutions in the region, and further, in securing funds for an initial three years; and as an interim measure, the Caribbean Research Centre, St Lucia, should be invited to house the centre;
3 that provision of training programmes of varying types and duration and at different levels should be organized and supported by governments;
4 that governments of the region recognize and support CARCAE as a visible organization serving adult education in the Caribbean, and further, that appropriate links with the CARICOM secretariat be established to give evidence of this regional support.

All of these recommendations have been fulfilled to varying extents, for example items 1, 2, and 4 have been almost fully accomplished, but 3 only partially so.

CARCAE's constitution

After five years and several drafts, the constitution for the Caribbean Regional Council for Adult Education was accepted by the First General Assembly held in Nassau, Bahamas, in April 1983. The aims and objectives of the council as prescribed in the constitution are

1 to promote and facilitate co-operation among national adult educational organizations and agencies in the non-Spanish-speaking territories amongst them;
2 to advance activities of members and to encourage co-operation amongst them;
3 to promote awareness and recognition of the importance of adult education and to seek and encourage adequate funding for this purpose from governments and other sources;

4 to initiate and/or to support conferences, seminars, training courses, workshops, research in the field of continuing education, the operation of a documentation centre, and a publication programme;

5 to advise governments and other relevant bodies on matters relating to adult education; and

6 to undertake such action and/or activities as the council may decide, in pursuance of the above.

The first executive body to be elected under the constitution included:

Honorary president:	Dennis Irvine (Jamaica)
Chairman:	Samuel Small (Guyana)
First vice-chairman:	Ralph Van Breet (Netherlands Antilles)
Second vice-chairman:	Hector Elizabeth (French Antilles)
Secretary-treasurer:	Esmond Ramesar (Trinidad and Tobago)
Assistant secretary-treasurer:	Colton Bennet (Barbados)
Member-at-large:	Louis Profitt (Guyana)
Executive member:	Edris Bird (Antigua/Barbuda)
Executive member:	Arthur Roach (Bahamas)
Executive member:	Simon Clarke (Jamaica)
Executive member:	Teresa Mason (St Lucia)

In order to promote CARCAE within the region, the chairman, while on a sabbatical from the University of Guyana, undertook, with a grant from Partners of the Americas, to visit each country and territory in the Caribbean which is a registered or potential member. While on tour he spoke with members of local adult education agencies, ministry officials, other related organizations, and assisted in conducting workshops/seminars on adult education.

CARCAE's representation at international meetings

In keeping with CARCAE's 1978 mandate, the council was represented at many regional, hemispheric, and international meetings. Some of the most important have been:

1 the 1979 ICAE general assembly and executive meeting held in Helsinki;

2   the 1980 ICAE executive meeting and seminar/workshop held in Washington, DC;

3   the 1980 St Lucia/Unesco meeting of experts from adult education institutions in the Caribbean held in Castries, St Lucia;

4   the 1980 Inter-American Federation of Adult Educators (FIDEA) First Regional Conference on Andragogy for the Caribbean area, held in Fort-de-France, Martinique;

5   the 1983 CARCAE general assembly and BAEA seminar/workshop on Action and Interaction in Formal and Non-Formal Education, held in Nassau, Bahamas;

6   the 1983 Unesco Major Project in the Field of Education for Latin America and the Caribbean, St John's, Antigua;

7   the 1983 Unesco Regional Technical Consultation on Adult Education within the Framework of the Fourth International Conference on Adult Education, Havana, Cuba;

8   the 1983 ICAE meeting and seminar/workshop on Adult Education and Culture, Baghdad, Iraq;

9   the 1984 CARCAE executive meeting and OSTICEBA seminar/workshop on the Adult Learner, Aruba, NA;

10 the 1984 ICAE executive meeting and conference on Adult Education and the Popularization of Science and Technology, Moscow, USSR;

11 the 1985 ICAE's International Meeting on Certification, Training, and Financing, Macau Association for Continuing Education (MACE), Macau;

12 the 1985 CARCAE executive meeting and seminar/workshop on Exchange of Innovative Experiences and Training of Specialists in Adult Education and Literacy in the English and Dutch-Speaking Countries of the Caribbean, Basseterre, St Christopher/Nevis;

13 the 1986 CARCAE/CREFAL/UWI seminar/workshop on Specific Support for Adult Education and Literacy Programmes, Kingstown, St Vincent;

14 the 1986 CARCAE'S second general assembly and seminar/workshop on Science and Technology: Implications for Education and Development, Port of Spain, Trinidad.

Country/Territorial Associations

The executive of CARCAE was very active in encouraging the establishment of adult education associations throughout the region. Prior to 1980 the only association in existence was the Adult Education Association of Guyana which was formed in 1957. To date the number has increased to include the following:

Adult Education Association of Guyana	(AEAG) – 1957
Congress of Adult Education of Trinidad and Tobago	(CAETT) – 1980
St Lucia Association of Continuing Education	(SLACE) – 1981
Adult Education Association of Barbados	(AEAB) – 1981
Jamaica Council for Adult Education	(JAMCAE) – 1982
Bahamas Adult Education Association	(BAEA) – 1982
Dominica Council for Adult Education	(DOMCAE) – 1983
Antigua and Barbuda Adult Education Association	(ABAEA) – 1983
St Kitts/Nevis Council for Adult Education	(SKNCAE) – 1984
Adult Education Council for Belize	(AECB) – 1984

Hopefully efforts are being made to establish associations in Grenada, Montserrat, St Vincent, the British Virgin Islands, and the Netherlands Antilles. CARCAE appears to have lost contact with Suriname and the French Antilles.

CLOSING REMARKS

The Caribbean Regional Council for Adult Education (CARCAE) elected a new executive at its last general assembly in April 1986. As a result the headquarters has shifted from the UWI St Augustine (Trinidad) Campus to UWI Cave Hill (Barbados) Campus. Samuel Small was re-elected chairman, with Patricia Ellis as secretary-treasurer.

The new executive has proposed a wide programme of activities, summarized below.

Regional meetings/seminars (general)

1 Three executive meetings cum regional seminars;
2 Tenth anniversary meeting;
3 Adult education and peace meeting of international peace network (ICAE).

Training

1 Continuation of the three-year certificate course in adult education;
2 Institution-building: strengthening of national associations and training workshops for leaders/members;
3 National needs assessment workshops and country workshops for different groups of adult educators, for example, administrators;
4 Training of trainers workshops.

Research

1 Participatory research network – national and regional workshops to share experiences and to explore research methods and techniques;
2 Publication of participatory research newsletters and case books;
3 Building a data base on adult education in the region by identifying, publishing, and disseminating findings of research which has been done, for example papers and studies prepared by both students in the Certificate Course and other researchers.
4 Literature search and other retrieval;
5 Building up a network of adult education researchers by identifying researchers/resource people for participatory research; organizing seminars for local participatory research co-ordinators and researchers in methods and techniques; and facilitating exchange visits for researchers within the region and with researchers in Latin America through CEAAL.

Documentation and communications

1 Establishing on a firmer base and expansion of the CARCAE's Communications Centre in St Lucia;
2 Production of a brochure on CARCAE and its work;
3 Production and publication of newsletters, series of occasional papers, and monographs;
4 Preparation of annotated bibliographies;
5 Preparation of directory of resource persons and agencies involved in adult education;

6 Facilitating exchange of information between adult educators and adult education agencies/institutions or agencies both within the region and internationally.

Literacy

1 A survey of literacy initiatives within the region;
2 Training of literacy facilitators;
3 Documentation of literacy experiences;
4 Seminars/workshops on literacy programming, planning, and evaluation.

REFERENCES

CARCAE (1983) *Report of Activities to General Assembly*, Nassau, Bahamas.
—— (1986) *Report of Activities to General Assembly*, Port-of-Spain, Trinidad.
—— (1987) *Outline of Programme Activities 1987–1989*, Barbados.
CARICOM (1982) *Final Report of C.F.T.C. Adviser to Caricom Education Project*, Georgetown, Guyana.
Clifford, A.B. (1984) 'An overview of the adult education situation in the English-speaking Caribbean', *OAS Regional Meeting on Adult Education and Technical Meeting on Integrated Adult Education*, San José, Costa Rica.
Ellis, P. (1985) *A Report of an Evaluation Study of the Three-Year Certificate Course for Adult Educators in the Non-Spanish-Speaking Caribbean*, University of the West Indies, St Augustine.
ICAE (1981) *Seminar Report on Adult Education, Training and Employment*, Port-of-Spain, Trinidad.
—— (1984) *National and Regional Adult Education Associations: A Survey of Member Organizations*, Toronto: OISE.
Lowe, J. (1975) *The Education of Adults: A World Perspective*, Paris/Toronto: Unesco.
Ramesar, E.D. (1983) 'Adult education in the Caribbean context: aspects of growth and consolidation under changing conditions', *Unesco Regional Technical Consultation on Adult Education within the Framework of the Fifth International Conference on Adult Education*, Havana.
—— (1985) 'Adult education: regional organizations in the Caribbean', *International Encyclopedia of Education*, vol.1, Oxford: Pergamon.
Ramesar, E.D. and Shorey, L. (1986) 'Roby Kidd and the Caribbean', in N.J. Cochrane *et al.* (eds) *J.R. Kidd: An International Legacy of Learning*, Centre for Continuing Education, University of British Columbia, Vancouver.

Report of First Regional Conference on Adult Education in the Caribbean (1952) Kingston, Jamaica.

Report of Second Regional Conference on Adult Education in the Caribbean (1970) Georgetown, Guyana.

Report on Third Regional Conference on Adult Education in the Caribbean (1977) Castries, St Lucia.

Unesco (1949) *Summary Report of the International Conference on Adult Education*, Paris: Unesco.

—— (1960) *World Conference on Adult Education: Final Report*, Paris: Unesco.

—— (1972) *Third International Conference on Adult Education: Final Report*, Paris: Unesco.

—— (1980) *Final Report on a Meeting of Experts for Adult Education Institutions in the Caribbean*, Castries, St Lucia.

—— (1983) *Final Report of the Seminar/Workshop on Adult Education and Literacy*, St John's, Antigua.

10

The Arab League Educational, Cultural, and Scientific Organization and adult education

Mohi Eldine Saber

INTRODUCTION

The Arab League Educational, Cultural, and Scientific Organization (ALECSO) is a specialized Arab organization established by the League of Arab States (LAS). Its primary responsibility is to promote and co-ordinate educational, cultural, and scientific activities at the Arab regional level and to help the Arab states to develop and implement new educational, cultural, and scientific development approaches and strategies that can meet the Arab world's needs and are commensurate with its realities and priorities.

The Arab League first decided to set up ALECSO in May 1964 but its practical establishment came into force on 25 July 1970. As an umbrella for the 'Joint Arab Work' in the field of education, it has become responsible for the development of the Arab adult education work as well as of the Arab adult education movement. To carry out this task, ALECSO has entrusted the issues of adult education to the Arab Literacy and Adult Education Organization (ARLO), one of its major organs and an independent entity.

ALECSO PURPOSES AND TARGETS

According to its constitution, ALECSO was established to attain 'unity of thought' among Arab countries through education, culture, and science and to raise the cultural standard of these countries so that they may pursue, catch up with, and contribute to world civilization. Within the framework of this overall objective, ALECSO has set for itself the following targets:

1   To work for the development of the Arab human resources by helping the Arab citizen to develop intellectually, morally, and culturally in such a way that would enable him to contribute to the build-up of his own society as well as to the human cultural heritage.

2   To provide the means of social, economic, and societal development in the Arab states to raise the standard of living at both individual and societal levels.

3   To effect progress in the factors affecting scientific development with a view to creating the appropriate atmosphere leading to the transfer of modern technology to the Arab world.

4   To improve development practices with a view to preserving Arab natural resources and rationalizing their use according to present and future needs of the Arab countries.

5   To exchange Arab thought and experience with other positive contemporary world ones within the context of the crucial issues facing the world such as the settlement of equitable peace, the security of human rights, and the establishment of a new just international order.

6   To develop Arab-Islamic culture at home in such a way that would make it contribute to world cultural development.

7   To seek the most effective ways and forms of participation in international endeavour for the development of mass media and communication as well as data processing, use, exchange, and documentation to facilitate their circulation in the service of the ALECSO objectives.

ADULT EDUCATION TASKS

As both alphabetical and cultural illiteracy constitute the major obstacle on the road to the comprehensive development of the Arab citizen, ALECSO devotes the greatest part of its adult education work to literacy work.

Priority is now given to achieve the following tasks:

1   Providing various Arab states with technical (and in some cases with material) assistance to launch comprehensive adult literacy campaigns according to the concepts and approaches adopted in the Arab Literacy Strategy.

2   Provision of the necessary well-trained cadres to carry out the

programmes, and the necessary aids, materials, and capabilities to implement the field-work.

3 Intensification of ALECSO programmes to pay attention to connecting literacy with the problems of the masses; meeting the needs of both individuals and communities, and the mobilizing of popular voluntary effort.

4 Development of studies and research on literacy legislations, effects of literacy on socio-economic development plans, and rationalization of educational systems in order to attain the standardization of compulsory education, and so on.

5 Development of literacy work's content and teaching methods in a bid to innovate their approaches and techniques within the framework of lifelong education, and the integration of formal and non-formal education.

6 Paying special attention to the educationally disadvantaged sectors, especially those who actually effect production such as the sectors of women, workers, and youth. These sectors should be given priority in literacy projects.

7 Articulating model all-out literacy informational campaigns to enable the Arab states to plan their informational campaigns on a methodological basis within the philosophy of the Arab Literacy Strategy.

8 Expansion of rural development programmes and connecting them with youth development projects and the introduction of modern practices in agricultural extension, co-operatives, vocational training, and bedouin resettlement projects.

9 Encouragement of academic research in the field of adult education carried out by institutes, colleges, and universities.

10 Introduction to the Arab world of broad adult education methodologies, concepts, approaches, and techniques and reactivating authentic inherited Arab adult education ones.

To make a systematic review of ALECSO's role and efforts in Arab adult education work and in the Arab adult education movement, it would be more appropriate in this essay to deal with the whole subject through its specialized organ, the Arab Literacy and Adult Education Organization (ARLO).

ARLO

ARLO was first established in 1966 within the secretariat of the Arab League. It was attached to ALECSO in 1970. ARLO's budget and programme are adopted by the Executive Council and General Conference of ALECSO. To achieve the general purposes of ALECSO, ARLO has the following functions to fulfil:

1 proposing and seeking the adoption of an Arab literacy and adult education strategy;
2 provision of co-ordination as far as literacy and adult education plans are concerned in the Arab states;
3 enabling the Arab states to elaborate unified literacy and adult education legislation;
4 organizing periodical conferences, expert meetings, symposia, seminars, and workshops to tackle problems and propose solutions;
5 maintaining co-operation with concerned international and regional organizations and associations;
6 organization and provision of scholarships;
7 exchange of experience, documents, and information with various Arab states and organizations;
8 provision of experts and technical requirements to carry out literacy and adult education programmes;
9 promotion of Arab national adult education associations and seeking the establishment of an Arab Adult Education Association;
10 carrying out a specialized publications and documentation programme;
11 conducting experiments, studies, and comparative research on the basic concepts and techniques related to literacy work and adult education.

BACKGROUND, PHILOSOPHY, AND STRATEGY

The Arab states represent an integrated community with a long history of common experiences, challenges, and hopes. In 1985 the total population of the Arab world was estimated at 193 million, or more than 4 per cent of the world's total population. Thus it comes fifth among world population groups next to China, India, the USSR, and the USA. The annual rate of population growth in the Arab world is 3.24, which is one of the highest rates in the world.

The economically active group of the population (15–60 years old) represents less than 50 per cent of the total population against

147

more than 60 per cent in the developed countries. Moreover, 7 per cent of the total population are still nomads or semi-nomads while about 63 per cent are rural and 30 per cent are urban.

Despite their classification into three economic groups (oil-rich, pastoral-agricultural, and multi-economic structure countries), all the Arab countries belong to the developing world so far as the economic and social structures are concerned.

Educationally the Arab world has in general achieved great strides in enrolment during the 1960s, 1970s, and the early 1980s. However, the most prominent problem has been the failure of Arab educational systems to readjust to reality, and to become an organic natural part of the texture of the society. They are still suffering from alienation. There are also the problems of making education authentic by assigning to it a role in community development and the problem of prevalent imbalance between social change factors and educational innovation.

Illiteracy represents the existing gap among the structure of the conventional societies and the nature of the educational systems resulting in the alienation of individuals. Statistical data of 1980 indicate that the overall rate of illiteracy in the Arab region was 60 per cent, and that it stood at 46 per cent for men and 74 per cent for women, whereas it is 30 per cent for the urban population against 70 per cent for rural people.

From an educational sociological point of view, the spread of illiteracy in such proportions throughout the Arab world means that the society is underdeveloped in its entire structure in comparison with the prevalent world cultural pattern. Therefore, illiteracy is not only an educational problem, but also a cultural one. It concerns both the underdevelopment of the society and the individual's ability to master the three Rs. The presence of the illiterate individual in a given society and his inability to exercise his full social life as far as production, consumption, and relations are concerned means that the structure of this society is a traditional one.

Accordingly a cultural review of the status of illiteracy in the Arab world revealed that there are two kinds of illiteracy: alphabetical illiteracy – the individual's inability to master the skills of reading, writing, and arithmetic; and cultural illiteracy – the underdevelopment of the society. The latter cannot be dealt with without resorting to a comprehensive confrontation with all aspects of social underdevelopment including alphabetical illiteracy.

This sociological conceptualization of the problems of illiteracy in the Arab world was fully reflected in the Arab Literacy Strategy adopted by all Arab states in Baghdad in 1976.

THE ARAB LITERACY STRATEGY

In its general concept the strategy is a framework of guidelines for action to help the Arab states formulate their respective comprehensive literacy plans.

The strategy objective is to emancipate people throughout the Arab world from both alphabetical and cultural illiteracy by raising them to such an educational and cultural level that enables them to

1   master the basic skills of reading, writing, and arithmetic to a level that qualifies them to continue their education and training; and
2   participate in the development and modernization of their community so as to provide the cultural and social atmosphere which motivates individuals to continue their education.

The strategy is based upon the principles of a comprehensive confrontation as an approach and the national campaign as a technique. In theory 'comprehensive confrontation' means that alphabetical literacy is not an end in itself. It cannot achieve the spontaneous development of the society.

Therefore the basis for literacy should be the confrontation of backwardness in all sectors of the society. Literacy should be just one of the tens of other activities carried out through a national campaign. Then illiterate people will have the opportunity to participate in the renovating of the functions of society if they continue their education. This approach would help bring about the comprehensive transformation of people and society, on the one hand, and overcome the traditional obstacles encountered in traditional literacy work carried out in evening voluntary classes such as dropping out and abstention on the other hand.

Within the framework of this concept, adult education has a radical role in effecting the process of transformation and activating of the structure of the traditional society along with literacy. These campaigns are being carried out in many Arab states by the joint efforts of both the official organs and bodies, and the local community resources and institutions within the framework of the concept of self-help.

149

ACTIVITIES OF ARLO

Although ARLO is quite concerned with the broad fields of adult education, adult literacy work has taken the first priority in its activities during the last ten years. Its programmes have been focused on

1 the explanation and propagation of the concepts and the scientific approaches included in the Arab Literacy Strategy;
2 translating its theoretical ideas into applicable procedural steps;
3 providing the Arab states with technical assistance in planning and implementing their national campaigns;
4 following-up the implementation of the strategy in various Arab states;
5 studying the obstacles and suggesting solutions;
6 the mobilization of popular organizations to take part in literacy campaigns; and
7 the preparation of prototype materials for literacy and post-literacy stages.

There follows a brief stocktaking of its main achievements during this period.

Meetings, conferences, and seminars

ARLO has organized two conferences. One of them was on the development of popular efforts in the fight against illiteracy. The other, the Fourth Alexandria Conference (Tunis 1984), was on the review of the Arab literacy work in the light of the implementation of the Arab Literacy Strategy. It also organized 15 symposia and seminars attended by 243 officials and 464 experts and observers. These meetings focused on the planning of literacy campaigns; the integration of literacy programmes in national development plans; adult education legislations; the use of media in literacy work; opening channels between formal and non-formal education; the cultural concept of literacy; lifelong education; the establishment of an Arab Open University; distance education; the obstacles hindering the implementation of the strategy; the concept and dimensions of popular participation; and the efforts of trade union and teachers' unions' leaders in literacy.

These meetings were designed to help Arab adult education leadership, at both high and middle levels, in how to implement the Arab Literacy Strategy, to conceive future work in broad adult education fields, and to exchange experiences in solving the field problems faced.

Workshops and camps

ARLO organized six workshops on literacy and post-literacy educational materials. These workshops were held in Jordan, Yemen, Sudan, Iraq, and Bahrain, and focused their work on how to develop the principles and specifications of literacy primers, post-literacy books, and neo-literate reading material such as adult magazines and hobby books. They were attended by eighty-five officials and experts.

In its endeavour to mobilize the efforts of youth, ARLO organized two Arab youth literacy camps in Somalia and Jordan. The camps were designed to help youth leaderships lay down a guide on how to organize youth participation in literacy work.

Training courses

The Arab Literacy campaigns have proved that there is an urgent need for mass training efforts for literacy teachers, instructors, and supervisors. The Iraqi campaign, for example, recruited 73,000 teachers within 18 months, while the Somali campaign made use of the efforts of 125 teachers and instructors. To meet this desperate need for trained cadres, ARLO designed a short 'intensive specialized training course'. To experiment and evaluate this course, ARLO experts implemented the model in more than twelve Arab countries in two phases. After evaluating the model, its documents were revised and published in a training guidebook. This guide is now used in many Arab states by literacy departments and training institutes.

Research and studies

During the period under review ARLO field research efforts were directed to tackling the problems facing the implementation of national literacy campaigns based on the strategy principles and concepts. A 'field operational village' was chosen in Egypt, Democratic Yemen, and Iraq to test the concepts and techniques stipulated in the Arab Literacy Strategy. This project covered a period of seven years and a host of positive results and lessons were learned and made use of in the field-work. ARLO experts, university staff members, and educational specialists took part in this project.

Other field research work was conducted on topics such as the diagnosis and measurement of illiterate people's motives to learn; the discovery and mobilization of spontaneous community leadership in literacy works; the quantitative and qualitative returns of literacy campaigns and their effect on productivity; the possibility of mobilizing traditional religious educational institutions in literacy work; and a feasibility study for the establishment of an Arab Open University.

Educational materials

In addition to the workshops meant to train Arab high-level cadres on the development of educational materials, ARLO has provided many Arab states with direct assistance in the preparation, development, evaluation, and – in some cases – the printing of their literacy primers. With regard to the preparation of post-literacy materials, ARLO has many endeavours. It continues to publish a series entitled 'The Adult's Literacy'. The booklets issued in this series are model reading materials for the new literates and national Arab agencies can make use of them or reprint them for their literacy classes' graduates.

ARLO also conducted an important phased field study on how to develop reading materials for the new literates. Two field surveys were applied in ten Arab states on the needs and on the available materials. Five prototype books were prepared, tested, evaluated, revised, and printed. The conclusions of this study were disseminated in various Arab states. The project was carried out in co-operation with the Arab Fund for Economic and Social Development (based in Kuwait).

In addition, ARLO has carried out projects to

1 prepare and publish a prototype issue of an adult magazine *AL-NOOR*;

2 produce an educational kit for adults;
3 prepare and produce model recorded lessons for illiterates in reading and arithmetic with the accompanying printed materials;
4 produce and prepare television, radio, and printed materials for a distance adult educational unit.

Popular participation

The Arab Literacy Strategy called for the mobilization of popular efforts and the encouragement of self-help and voluntary work in the fight against illiteracy. In response, ARLO organized a symposium on the dimensions and concept of popular participation and a conference on the development of popular efforts in literacy work. ARLO also established two models for popular participation in Morocco and among the Palestinians in Lebanon.

ARLO has a continuing project to extend technical and material assistance to the organizations and popular agencies which are concerned with literacy. Twenty-five Arab organizations have made use of this assistance.

In addition, ARLO has sought to help the Arab states establish the Arab Adult Education Association. A meeting of experts was held to compose its constitution. It is expected to hold a constitutional conference to announce the association in the near future.

Information and documentation

ARLO has its specialized journal in adult education, the *Education of the Masses*; it appears in Arabic with an English supplement. Though its main topics are focused on literacy and adult education in the Arab homeland, it also covers international adult educational trends and innovations.

ARLO's publications programme includes the publication of translated and specially written books on adult education, neo-literates' model books, and books collating the studies presented to ARLO conferences, seminars, and symposia.

On the occasion of the Arab Literacy Day (8 January) ARLO publishes informational materials (posters, films, brochures, booklets, and so on). These materials are designed to help the Arab bodies to raise the awareness of people towards the problems of illiteracy.

With regard to the documentation and exchange of information in the field of adult education, ARLO has a specialized information network equipped with modern technical means of processing and exchanging information. The network has its yearbook and has issued union catalogues about the specialized books and magazines in various Arab Libraries. ARLO has a specialized adult education library in its headquarters in Baghdad.

THE ARAB LITERACY FUND

The general conference of ALECSO approved the establishment of the Arab Fund for Literacy and Adult Education in 1979. The fund's board of directors was formed in 1981 and it has begun its activities since then. The purpose of the fund is to take part in financing the plans of universal compulsory education as well as literacy and adult education projects in the Arab states within the framework of the Arab Literacy Strategy.

The resources of the fund consist of

1 the allocations earmarked for it in the ALECSO budget;
2 voluntary contributions by the Arab states;
3 contributions of Arab and international organizations, bodies, and institutions;
4 contributions of individuals; and
5 revenues from the fund's deposits.

The fund initially developed a national plan to cover its activities in an integrated form. The first stage of this plan had four programmes for educational innovations, technical assistance, technological requirements, and financial assistance. The present phase of the fund's work is mainly concerned with the establishment of a solid basis for its future work, that is an infrastructural stage.

Work has already begun on many of its projects. One of these projects is the production of a joint Arab television literacy programme (AN-ALAWAN) to be transmitted through the Arab Satellite (Arabsat). The programme's educational materials are based upon the 'cultural concept'. In addition to teaching the three

Rs, it provides the learners with a broad basis of cultural information about their circumstances, and the means to develop themselves, about concepts like national development, citizenship, and participation in community development, about their living conditions, and so on.

ALECSO FIELD TRAINING CENTRES

In addition to ARLO, ALECSO has two training centres for adult education cadres. The first is sited in Tripoli (Libya) and serves the Arab states in North Africa, that is Libya, Algeria, Tunisia, Morocco, and Mauritania. The other is sited in Bahrain and serves the Arab Gulf states, that is Bahrain, Kuwait, Qatar, Oman, Saudi Arabia, Iraq, United Arab Emirates, and both Yemens. ALECSO makes use of Shindi centre in Sudan to train the field cadres of remaining Arab states.

The centres are financed from ALECSO's budget and their programmes are approved by the general conference of ALECSO. They are meant to provide residential training courses to field literacy and adult education cadres in their respective regions of the Arab homeland. They organize three-month training courses for field and middle-level cadres in their headquarters. Furthermore, they hold extensive special training courses for the field cadres of any state at its demand to meet its urgent needs.

They also organize specialized courses on audio-visual aids, planning, and so on, as well as special training courses for leaders of popular organizations in literacy and adult education.

The Tripoli and Bahrain centres extend technical expertise to adult education departments. They also conduct field research work on the problems facing literacy and adult education work in their respective member states. In addition, they have their specialized journals and their publications programmes.

ALECSO also has its Arab Centre for Educational Technology (based in Kuwait). In addition to its broad tasks in the service of formal education, the centre carries out projects especially designed to serve adult education. It extends technical assistance to ARLO projects which have technological components. Recorded lessons for adults, educational kits, and other research work on adult educational techniques are also carried out by the centre.

155

ALECSO IN THE FIELD

Through its specialized organs, ALECSO has extended to Arab adult educationalists and officials a wide range of meeting opportunities to exchange experience and options and to lay down the scientific basis for the implementation of the Arab Literacy Strategy. Within ARLO programmes alone, meetings were held, 150 papers were presented, and 780 officials and experts participated. In addition, field training was extended to 405 senior adult education trainers and more than 2,000 instructors.

ALECSO has also facilitated field-level exchange of experience through a programme specially articulated to encourage visits between various directors of Arab national adult education departments. Similar efforts were exerted by ALECSO to help Arab adult education officials attend important international adult education events such as the Fourth International Adult Educational Conference (Paris 1985) and the Paris and Buenos Aires Conferences organized by the International Council for Adult Education (1982–5).

With regard to the exchange of experience with concerned bodies at the international level, ALECSO has had a good working relationship with Unesco and its organs in the field of adult education. There is a detailed programme of joint projects and exchanges of experience between both organizations.

ALECSO and ARLO are active members of the International Council for Adult Education (ICAE) and ALECSO's director-general is vice-president of ICAE; there are also numerous relations with regional adult educational bodies and associations.

Many Arab states have witnessed the implementation of national comprehensive literacy campaigns during the past eight years. There was the Iraqi campaign (1978), the campaign of Kuwait (1981), the campaign of the Arab Republic of Yemen (1983), the Democratic Yemen Campaign (1984), and the Palestinian campaign (1982). There are also campaigns in Syria, Bahrain, Sudan, and Morocco.

Through ARLO, ALECSO has participated in all preparatory steps taken to launch these campaigns starting from planning to the preparation of educational materials. Technical assistance was also extended in fields like training, audio-visual aids, and so on.

In addition, ALECSO has earmarked allocations in its regular budget to provide these campaigns with technical and material assistance. ALECSO experts have had a vital role in following up these campaigns and providing them with technical assistance as the need arises.

PERSPECTIVES

Within ALECSO's medium plan for the period 1982–96 adult education efforts will be focused on

1   studying the present Arab practices in the fields of literacy and adult education and analysing them with a view to laying down the most appropriate techniques to ensure the implementation of the Arab Literacy Strategy;
2   ensuring continuity of work with regard to the establishment of Arab national adult education institutions;
3   evaluating national literacy and adult educational plans in the light of ongoing practices;
4   reinforcement of ARLO's adult education information network and linking it with similar international networks;
5   elaborating a masterplan for continuing education in the Arab homeland;
6   institutionalizing cultural dialogues with the world in the field of adult education;
7   making an effective contribution to the world thought in adult education.

TOWARDS ADULT EDUCATION PLANS

New adult educational needs have strikingly emerged in the Arab states that have witnessed national literacy campaigns. More than 2 million new literates have graduated from literacy classes in Iraq, Kuwait, and the two states of Yemen alone.

To meet these increasing needs for adult educational opportunities ARLO programmes for the next five years will lay stress on planning for an adult continuing education strategy for the Arab states. In addition, ARLO will extend technical assistance to a number of Arab states in articulating their post-literacy adult educational systems. There are plans in Iraq and Democratic Yemen to found systematic non-formal adult education systems.

157

The main features of both planned systems centre on continuing education, training, and mass culture.

Continuing education

To meet the needs of new literates, parallel adult formal education facilities have been conceived to provide them in their leisure time with formal primary, secondary, and, in some cases, university education.

Training

These plans provide a wide range of vocational, technical, and professional training opportunities for adults at large.

Mass culture

This focuses on the use of mass media, theatres, museums, and so on, in adult education.

EXPECTED DEVELOPMENTS

ALECSO – as a tool of Arab work in adult education – has already started a process of evaluating its work and developing new paths in adult education. The following is a brief review of some of these developments.

The use of distance education techniques

Through ARLO, ALECSO has organized two events on distance education. A symposium was held on distance education techniques and a feasibility study was conducted on the possibility of establishing an Arab Open University. Prototype material and pilot projects on some aspects of distance educational techniques are already in production or under development.

The Arab satellite educational programmes have been referred to ALECSO to propose, pilot production, experiment, and plan.

With regard to adult education, a plan was presented on how and what to transmit to meet adult educational needs. ARLO was authorized to produce a prototype programme on the adult distance educational unit. These developments are expected to continue and expand.

Popular participation and self-help trend

The development of the popular participation movement in literacy and adult education has been latterly one of the main concerns of ALECSO. This movement has already been embodied in many Arab self-help initiatives and in some material contributions through the Arab Literacy Fund. It is expected to develop into a mass popular movement to self-finance many adult education projects. The fund's national finances will play an important role in mobilizing resources for it. The next few years will also witness the establishment of the Arab Adult Education Association to co-ordinate and encourage popular efforts in the field of adult education.

Research and studies

In addition to the ongoing and planned field research and studies, ARLO research work is expected to centre on confirming the Arab andragogy and putting adult education work in tune with modern international developments making use of educational technology and other world experience. There will also be a wide range of experimentation and pilot projects on the use of new innovative techniques in training and developing training guides. Research work is also expected to expand in the use of distance educational techniques, especially with regard to the use of correspondence education and self-help education materials, in adult rural education institutions, in the education of women, and in such groups as the nomads and fishermen.

Documentation and exchange

ALECSO has already developed its main information network in Tunis. However, it has also established an adult education information network in ARLO headquarters in Baghdad. The network has been equipped with modern processing and distribution facilities. During the next few years it will have centres in all Arab states. Future plans see an automatic linkage with similar world networks. The Arab Literacy Fund also has a project to establish an Arab adult education publications house to provide the Arab states with much-needed works in adult education and literacy.

CONCLUSION

As an inter-governmental organization responsible among other things for the Arab Joint Work in the field of education, ALECSO – through its specialized organ ARLO – plays a key role in the development of adult education in the Arab homeland, both in theory and in practice. In addition, it helps concerned Arab governmental and non-governmental organizations plan, carry out, co-ordinate, and evaluate their contributions to the Arab adult education movement. At the international level, ALECSO establishes and maintains working and exchange channels with almost all international governmental and non-governmental bodies working in adult education.

Though the allocations for ARLO programmes and projects are derived from the ALECSO biennial budget, determined efforts have been recently exerted to mobilize out-of-budget financial resources to finance out-of-programme projects aiming at pushing forward the Arab adult education movement and to provide funds for essential adult literacy and primary education projects in the least developed countries.

ALECSO has led the Arab joint efforts to determine priority fields of work in adult education, to lay down and adopt strategies for the generalization of primary and adult basic education, and to provide technical, human, and financial resources to adult education departments in various Arab states.

First priority is given, at the present time, to the eradication of cultural illiteracy among the educationally deprived sectors of the Arab society. Nevertheless, ALECSO pays increasing attention to the development of other adult educational concepts, activities, innovations, techniques, approaches, and materials within the framework of lifelong education.

In a word, ALECSO and its organ ARLO (being the Arab

clearing-house in adult education) have fulfilled their role in the Arab adult education work with regard to the development of strategies, the laying down of plans, the training of cadres, the design of working guides, the production of prototype materials, and so on. In response, the Arab field-work has recently made real strides in the shape of comprehensive literacy campaigns, pilot adult educational projects in the fields of distance education, extra-mural studies, and so on. As a result of the comprehensive literacy campaigns based upon the principles of the Arab Literacy Strategy, millions of new literates have graduated and have joined the mainstream of lifelong education in Iraq, Kuwait, Bahrain, the two Yemens, Somalia, Sudan, and Syria. There are systematic efforts to meet their new educational needs and ALECSO experts are also there taking part in the cycle of innovation.

Index